On Foreign Assignment

❖❖❖❖❖❖❖❖❖❖❖❖❖❖❖❖❖❖❖

The Inside Story
of
Journalism's Elite Corps

Ab Douglas

Detselig Enterprises Ltd.
Calgary, Alberta

On Foreign Assignment:
The Inside Story of Journalism's Elite Corps

© 1993 Ab Douglas

Canadian Cataloguing in Publication Data

Douglas, Ab.
  On foreign assignment

  ISBN 1-55059-057-X
  1. Foreign correspondents. 2. Foreign
news. I. Title.
PN4784.F6D67 1993   070.4'332   C93-091393-0

Detselig Enterprises Ltd.
210, 1220 Kensington Road NW
Calgary, Alberta T2N 3P5

Printed in Canada   SAN 115-0324

This book is dedicated to Rick, Barb and Ted

Contents

Acknowledgements

The idea for this book originated with my journalism students at the University of Regina. Almost without exception they showed a keen interest in foreign reporting. I suspect that much of the glamor and adventure they associated with this particular field of journalism came from the movies and television.

When I suggested checking out the libraries for more substantive information on the subject, we found that except for some personal anecdotes contained in the memoirs of retired correspondents, there was little to be found.

One of my students asked, "Why don't you write a book?"

Well, it took a while, but I did. And just as John Donne found that no man is an island unto himself, I discovered that no book is the product of a single mind.

In my case, there are many people I am indebted to. There's the late Matthew Halton. But for him, the journalistic seed might never have been planted in my mind. It was this Albertan from Pincher Creek whose vivid wartime radio reports, complete with battle sounds, brought the cataclysmic events wracking Europe into our remote rural community. As a boy growing up on a Manitoba farm, these CBC radio reports were often my only source of war news, because we seldom got to see a current newspaper or magazine.

If Halton was the inspiration, James M. Minifie was a major influence in my maturation as a reporter. Don, as he was known to his friends, was an urbane transplanted Saskatchewanian who seemed to move effortlessly through Washington's corridors of power. His reports, whether for his paper *The New York Herald Tribune* or for CBC radio, were invariably incisive, uncompromising and always well sourced.

Little did I realize during my early years as a novice reporter that Don would one day be one of my colleagues in the CBC foreign correspondent corps, and that Matthew Halton's son David and I would work together on the Corporation's European beat.

Most of the experiences, observations and anecdotes on these pages are taken from my accumulated notes, script files and from recollections of the numerous stories exchanged among my correspondent confreres while on assignments from Belfast to Baghdad, Vienna to Vladivostok. A special thank you to all of them.

For access to archival material I owe thanks to the National Archives in Ottawa, Scripps Howard Newspaper Alliance, The Ernie Pyle Archives in Indianapolis, The Times of London, The International Federation of Journalists in Brussels and The Alberta Historical Society.

For case histories of the dangers and harassment faced by today's correspondents in various parts of the world, I appreciate the efforts of Jan Ellis and Pam Scholman at the New York offices of the Committee to Protect Journalists. Similar assistance was provided by the International Press Institute in London.

I am indebted to Martin Brech of Mahopac, New York, formerly of the U.S. Army's 14th Infantry Regiment, for an eyewitness account of the treatment of German prisoners at the end of WW II.

Thanks also to Dixie Lorentz, Charlene Brummund and Jan Olechowski for their patience and dedication in typing the numerous drafts in the preparation of the manuscript.

Cartoons are reprinted with the permission of Brian Gable, *The Globe & Mail*; Cam Cardow, *Regina Leader Post*; Dale Cummings, *Winnipeg Free Press*; Adrian Raeside, *Victoria Times-Colonist*; and Denny Pritchard, *Ottawa Citizen*.

Detselig Enterprises Ltd. appreciates the financial assistance for its 1993 publishing program from Canada Council and The Alberta Foundation for the Arts (a beneficiary of the Lottery Fund of the Government of Alberta).

Introduction

PEOPLE AND EVENTS BEYOND OUR BORDERS HAVE LONG
fascinated us.

A thousand years BC, the Greeks were entranced by Homer's *Iliad* and
Odyssey. Based on legend, the epic works told stories of the Trojan war,
of Helen of Troy (the face that launched a thousand ships) and tales of
the circuitous return of the Greek heroes after the fall of Troy.

At a time when our ancestors rarely ventured beyond a 15 kilometre
radius of their birthplace, the world beyond held a combination of terror
and fascination. Those with the courage and adventurism to strike out
into the great unknown became the stuff of heroes and legends.

Marco Polo was such a man. He was, in fact, the world's first "foreign
correspondent," although he would not have considered himself a journalist, nor indeed understood the term. A merchant prince of Venice, Polo
was a Middle Ages adventurer with the ability and inclination to put down
on paper all he had seen and experienced during his travels through the
far eastern realms of Kublai Khan—China and Japan.

After 17 years of roaming throughout Southeast Asia, Polo settled
down in 1296 to begin a chronicle of his travels. His journal was much
more than a mere recounting of tales of adventure and strange foreign
customs. He reported such oddities as paper currency, asbestos, coal and
other phenomena still largely unknown in Europe.

For all the enlightenment of the Renaissance, Polo's "reports" remained the chief Western source of information on the Far East for
hundreds of years.

Significant additional material on the far-flung corners of the Asian
continent did not become available until the late nineteenth century.

News from the "new worlds" of the Americas came from other
adventurers- cum-men of letters like Antonis Pigafetta who sailed around
the world with Magellan's expedition. And Sir Walter Raleigh who had
a way with words as well as the ladies. No one knows for sure whether
the gallant Englishman actually laid his fancy cloak over a muddy
walkway for his Queen. We do know that the luckless Sir Walter, who
eventually lost his head in the Tower of London, wrote extensively about
his "voyage of discovery" to the New World.

By the early nineteenth century the value of this abstract commodity
called "news" was becoming apparent—at least to a far-sighted few.

vv

One of these was the head of the London-based Rothschild dynasty. Nathan Meyer Rothschild realized early on that economic acumen alone could not sustain a financial empire. Rothschild had already established an efficient domestic information service, but it was no longer enough. The world was shrinking even then. What happened beyond England's shores had a direct impact on its economy and politics. Rothschild knew he needed information from abroad if he was to make intelligent business decisions and stock market transactions.

In the summer of 1815 the London Stock Exchange was teetering on the brink of collapse. On the continent, the armies of Britain and France, the two superpowers of the day, were squaring off against each other on the fields of Waterloo. The British were under the command of the aristocratic Duke of Wellington, the French under Napoleon. It would be weeks before news of the battle's outcome could reach London. In spite of help from the Prussians, a victory for Wellington was far from assured. A British defeat would send stock prices plummeting. A victory would send them soaring. Nervous investors could only sit and wait, or panic and dump stock. One stock holder who wasn't chewing his nails was Nathan Meyer Rothschild.

Rothschild organized his own foreign news service. He sent a reporter to Waterloo to find out who won. Using a system of couriers on horse back, a fast ship and carrier pigeons, news of Wellington's victory over Napoleon reached Rothschild within hours. While other members of the Exchange faced the prospect of financial ruin, Rothschild calmly bought up the shares of frightened investors. In a single day he made a fortune and at the same time saved the London Exchange from collapse. The case for fast, efficient international news coverage had been made.

It would be another 35 years before that need would be met in any kind of organized way. The year after Rothschild's mounted couriers galloped from Waterloo to Calais, Paul Julius Reuter was born at Kassel, Germany. As a young man he became intrigued with the newly invented telegraph. Reuter was quick to grasp the commercial importance of Samuel Morse's dots and dashes as a new way to carry news, supplementing, if not replacing, the cumbersome system of riders, ships, pigeons and coaches. He founded the Reuter Telegraph Company and tried to start the world's first news agency in Paris. The French weren't interested, so Reuter moved to London where he opened a news office and persuaded English newspaper editors to publish his telegrams of events on the Continent.

In time he had an information network linking England, Germany and France. The rest, as they say, is history. Today, *Reuters* news agency spans the globe. Its reputation is such that it is the only foreign-based news agency to be given equal status with American-owned *Associated*

vv

Press and *United Press International* at U.S. presidential news conferences.

The telegraph, however, did not immediately retire the carrier pigeons to their lofts. Telegraphs, and later telephones, needed wires and the world wasn't yet "wired" as it is today. Almost a hundred years to the day after Morse sent his "What hath God wrought" message on the telegraph, war correspondents on the beaches of Normandy were using pigeons to send back their dispatches on the D-Day landings with less than spectacular results.

Charles Lynch, a Canadian reporter working for *Reuters,* recalls that he released 36 birds two at a time, one male and one female, in hopes that they would head to their home lofts in England, from where news of the allied landings would reach the world. Lynch didn't have much luck. His pigeons all headed, not across the channel, but straight for the enemy lines in the general direction of Berlin. Romanticism dies hard.

Nevertheless, the idea of pigeons as news carriers has so intrigued correspondents over the years that anyone who carries out news dispatches or tapes for reporters with transmission difficulties is still referred to as a "pigeon." This human variety is usually a student, diplomat or tourist flying out of areas where journalists work under severe restrictions. The pigeoning system is an entrenched code of conduct within the reporting fraternity itself—especially in war time. Competition between television networks and news agencies is always fierce, but in tight situations it is understood that the reporter moving out to a communication facility "pigeons" out competitors' tapes and dispatches. That isn't as vital as it once was.

Barring government restrictions, a globe-girdling maze of space age technology now keeps correspondents in constant contact with their editors from whichever corner of the world they find themselves. Today, Rothschild's correspondent at the Battle of Waterloo could use a portable satellite uplink to transmit the battle's results and even live pictures of the battle to a waiting world.

Modern technology has forced governments and the media to reevaluate the very meaning of freedom of information. Would live pictures of combat represent the reality of war or an illusion of reality? Does the combination of democracy and television make waging war impossible? Can governments conduct deliberate and responsible diplomacy if they communicate instantaneously via the media's satellite party line? When censorship makes it impossible to report the "whole truth," is it better to report part of the truth than no truth at all?

International reporting is considerably more complex today than it was when Reuter tapped out the first snippets of news on his telegraph.

vvv

One thing, however, hasn't changed. That is the role of the foreign correspondent. He or she still has to get the story and get it out, often from nearly inaccessible locations in vast territories, or from the front lines of battle. The job calls for the stamina of a mule. The pace is brutal, the food often inedible and the water undrinkable. Airport and customs guards can be bullying, politicians and government leaders self-serving and manipulative. And there's enough danger to send the adrenalin into overdrive a good deal of the time. There's also a dash of glitz and glamor. Roll it all together and you've got the most exciting job in journalism.

Few foreign correspondents willingly turn in their trench coats. Former *Southam* reporter Peter Calami probably speaks for most correspondents when he suggests that those of us who do come in from the cold still flaunt our battered Burberrys as a quiet boast that we once earned our way "in the most elite corps of journalism." For us, getting the story was a story in itself.

The War Watchers

> The ancients had a great advantage over us in that their armies were not trailed by a second army of pen pushers.
>
> — Napoleon

The Crimean War

MOWBRAY MORRIS, MANAGER OF THE *TIMES OF LONDON,* and his editor John Delane were beside themselves. It was 1854, war had just broken out in the Crimea, and as so often happens when wars start, it was popular. In Queen Victoria's words "popular beyond belief." There was a voracious appetite for news which *The Times* could not supply because it had no reporter on the scene.

In those days, British editors scrounged war news where they could find it, by scalping continental newspapers, repeating rumors or hiring junior officers as "stringers." Journalism was more advanced in continental Europe, as Napoleon's frustration with the press indicated. These officers were of course soldiers first and reporters second. Not surprisingly their "reports" in the form of letters or diaries were heavily biased. Understandably, these men had no appreciation of what constituted "news." That was the frustrating situation *The Times* faced with its stringer in the Crimea, a young artillery lieutenant who apparently kept a meticulous diary, but planned to send it in when the fighting was over.

Delane decided it was time to send his own man to the front. (There was still no such thing as formal accreditation to the military.) His man was William Howard Russell who would go on to cover half a dozen other nineteenth century battles, ranging from the obscure dust up between Schleswig-Holstein and Denmark, to the Zulu uprising in South Africa, to the American Civil War.

Russell was breaking new journalistic ground. His first reports were simply letters to his editor, but it must be said that what he lacked in style he made up for in content. He didn't mince words. The vaunted British Army, he wrote, was in terrible shape—poorly-equipped and poorly-led by the aristocratic officer class of the day. The human suffering was indescribable. Another reporter, working out of Turkey for the rival *London Daily News,* came to the same conclusion. Needless to say, this double-barrelled assault didn't go down well with the military. The reporters' observations, though, were to prove tragically accurate. In the meantime the British commander-in-chief, Lord Raglan, would have

vv

nothing to do with war correspondents. Russell was treated like a pariah. He was constantly harassed, forced into the company of the camp followers and obliged to live off the land as best he could.

In spite of such seemingly insurmountable obstacles, Russell's dispatches got back to London. As his stature grew at home, his relations with the army improved, but only slightly. The die had been cast. The relationship between war correspondent and the military would be uneasy at best, hostile at worst and to the everlasting shame of the profession of journalism, sink at times into abject sycophancy.

American Civil War

If the Crimea was the pioneering ground for combat reporting, it was the American Civil War approximately ten years later that gave birth to the modern war correspondent. The telegraph was in general use and photography was coming into its own. Newspapers still did not have the technology to reproduce photos, but photographers like Matthew Brady provided a voluminous pictorial record of the greatest single event in American history. Equipment was cumbersome and "film" speed slow. Most of the pictures were posed or taken after the event. It has now been determined that the famous photograph of the dead Confederate sharpshooter at Little Round Top was posed. Experts are convinced that a dead soldier was moved to the spot and a rifle carefully placed in a leaning position against the pile of rocks.

The calibre of reporting on both sides was abysmal. The war attracted hundreds of reporters who were more adventurers than journalists. Reporting was consequently of a sensational nature with larger issues of graft, corruption and incompetence of the leadership largely ignored. Some correspondents moonlighted by taking military administration jobs, thus hopelessly compromising themselves. Reports from both sides were highly propagandistic, the South somewhat more so because most of its news came from Confederate officers who acted as stringers for their local papers.

One can only imagine how the war would have turned out if television had been on the scene. It was years before the public learned of the true cost, 620 thousand dead, more Americans dead than in WW I, WW II, Korea and Vietnam combined.

The entire profession of journalism was still in its infancy. Basic standards of ethics, balance and objectivity were almost entirely absent. The war was accentuated by these shortcomings.

Almost by accident though, it did introduce a fundamental change in the way news reports are written. The classic chronological style of reporting, which built up to the climax at the end of the story, was scrapped out of necessity. Time on the telegraph line was limited,

vv

expensive and uncertain. Nothing was more frustrating for the reporter, who may have ridden all night to get to a telegraph station, than to have the line go dead just as he was getting to the essential part of his story. So, the new lead was born. Stories were tightened up so that the first few sentences contained the basic elements of what, who, where, when and why—the 5 W's of journalism. Details were then added in descending order of importance. The style endures to this day.

Correspondents are often too close to the event to fully appreciate its historical significance. So it was with the American Civil War. No better example can be given than Lincoln's Gettysburg Address. The dedication of the National Cemetery at Gettysburg was treated in a most routine way by the press of the day and so was the president's famous "four score and seven years" speech. Several reporters kissed off their Gettysburg dispatches with the words, "the president also spoke."

For all its shortcomings, war reporting was here to stay. Readers had developed an insatiable appetite for war stories and the profit hungry press was determined to provide it. There was no shortage of volunteers for the job from the reporter ranks. An *Associated Press* reporter was with General George Custer at the battle of Little Big Horn and correspondents descended in ever increasing numbers to cover the Franco-Prussian War, the Russo-Japanese War, the Boer War and scores of lesser conflicts in between. When there wasn't a real war going on, newspaper owners weren't above trying to invent one.

Spanish-American War

In New York, William Randolph Hearst's *Journal* was in a circulation war with Joseph Pulitzer's *World. The Journal's* star reporter, Richard Davis, was in Cuba covering that colony's struggle for independence from Spain. Hearst was itching to get the United States into the war. He sent an artist to Cuba to illustrate the dispatches from Davis. The story goes that the artist found nothing of news value to draw and informed Hearst accordingly:

> *All quiet. No trouble.*
> *No war. Wish to return.*

Hearst responded:

> *Stay.*
> *You furnish pictures.*
> *I will furnish war.*

World War I

War reportage reached its low point in more ways than one during World War I, "the war to end all wars." British, as well as foreign papers wanting to cover the action were met with an uncompromising "No" from

vv

the British High Command. Nor did the press get any encouragement from the politicians, including Winston Churchill who had himself been a correspondent during the Boer War and was now First Lord of the Admiralty. The government thought it quite satisfactory for the military to prepare regular communiqués for direct distribution to the papers for publication without change. Once these communiqués had appeared in the British press they would be sent along to Canadian and other colonial newspapers.

The press rebelled. Unsanctioned correspondents were sent to the Continent to pick up stories as best they could without military co-operation. There was no shortage of volunteers, but it was a risky business. The army warned that any correspondent found lurking near the front would be shot. The French army was only slightly more co-operative. (The Germans also banned correspondents from the front, but conducted regular press conferences and issued official communiqués.)

This cat and mouse game on the Allied side became intolerable for both military and press. The army decided to end the chaos. Correspondents were thoroughly vetted, slapped into uniform and given official accreditation to the forces. Action coverage was carried out on a pooling basis. Names were put in a hat and those drawn reported on the fighting in their designated area, sharing the information with their colleagues.

Censorship was stifling, with the result that the readers back home got little more than reports of heroism, gallantry and glory—a sure formula for keeping recruits coming. There was no hint of the calamitous casualties in the trenches and mud holes nor the incompetence of those in command. The free-wheeling American press was also brought abruptly into line when their country entered the war. They could no longer report from the German side and were subject to the same rigorous censorship as the British and French correspondents.

Canadian historian Jack Granatstein has described WW I as an "arguably imperialist conflict." There were no great issues at stake which justified the slaughter of a whole generation of young men. Incompetent commanders sent hundreds of thousands of their troops to certain death for the sake of a few yards of mud. Had this war been televised like Vietnam it wouldn't have lasted as long as it did. This is not to say that the public had no reservations. The casualties were too enormous to hide. Entire battalions often drawn from a single community were wiped out. Whatever their reservations, people kept their thoughts to themselves, and there wasn't a peep of protest from the press. Canadian papers dutifully echoed the official line of an unquestioning, loyal colonial government.

vv

When the war ended, a numbed populace (Canada with a population of less than 10 million had lost 75 000 men) was treated to more patriotic platitudes. Typical was this paragraph from the *Edmonton Bulletin*, paying tribute to one of the city's returning regiments.

> *From the very commencement of hostilities the men (of the 19th Alberta Dragoons) inspired by patriotic devotion, offered themselves almost as one for the service of the flag.*

There was no questioning of what had actually been achieved at horrendous cost.

British war correspondent Sir Phillip Gibb summed up the confused and contradictory thinking of the day. "Some of us wrote the truth from the first to the last—apart from the naked realism of horrors and losses and criticism of the facts, which did not come within the liberty of our pen."

It is difficult for reporters covering conflict to stay emotionally neutral. Invariably professional judgment becomes clouded by emotion. Reporters covering the Arab states often sympathize with the Palestinian cause, while those based in Israel tend to lean toward the Israeli political line. Recognizing the fact that a reporter's work may be influenced by emotion, the *New York Times* for some time did not assign Jewish reporters to Israel. This tendency to take sides was carried to extremes during the Spanish Civil War where such illustrious personalities as Ernest Hemingway, Martha Gellhorn (later Hemingway's wife), Arthur Koestler and Jim Lardner wrote from the Republican side. All were totally committed to the leftist cause. They exaggerated Nationalist atrocities while conveniently overlooking similar conduct on their side. (Reporters with General Franco's forces did likewise.)

Forty years after the war, Martha Gellhorn told author Phillip Knightley that "any dispassionate objective reports might get the facts right but not capture the emotion, the commitment, the feeling that we were all in it together, the certainty that we were right."

George Orwell went further. The one-time British journalist, and author of *1984* charged that coverage of the Spanish Civil War was the worst he had ever seen. "Early in life," he wrote, "I had noticed that no event is ever correctly reported in a newspaper, but in Spain, for the first time, I saw newspaper reports which did not bear any relation to the facts, not even the relationship which is implied in an ordinary lie."

The evidence is unmistakable. In this war, professional judgment was overwhelmed by emotion.

This certainty of the rightness and the inevitable triumph of the leftist cause had its beginnings in the Russian Revolution. Here, for the first time, political ideology intruded on the military and the old blood, guts

vvv

and glory school of reporting wasn't up to the task of informed analysis. Western correspondents sent to cover the revolution were woefully ignorant of the ideological, social and economic forces that were convulsing a nation and shaking the world. Marxism, leftist political thought, communism, were foreign words and concepts in journalistic circles. Few correspondents even bothered to report on Lenin's arrival in Russia after his historic journey from Switzerland through Germany in a sealed railway car.

By default it was left to a handful of pro-Bolshevik journalists, like American John Reed, to define the issues. Their sympathies were by their own admission not neutral, but they did see the historical significance of what was happening and tried to tell the story with what Reed called, "the eye of a conscientious reporter, interested in setting down the truth." Reed's book *Ten Days That Shook The World*, though clearly sympathetic to the communist cause, is still essential reading for the serious student of international political science.

World War II

In the aftermath of WW I and the revolution in Russia, a tell-it-all-the-way-it-is school of reporting emerged in the United States. Truth and objectivity were to be the bywords, come what may. Such a brave new world of journalism was to prove more elusive than anyone thought.

"It was propaganda—everything done by all of us was propaganda, though we might not have admitted it, or even realized it at the time." With that sweeping statement—veteran journalist Charles Lynch dismissed his news dispatches and those of his colleagues during World War II. Certainly news coverage of the war was devoted almost exclusively to galvanizing public support for the war effort. Censorship was for the most part uncompromising and for the first time reporters were skilfully stage-managed by newly-established military public relations units. All this was done with the consent and compliance of the media. But to label all coverage as distortions and half-truths aimed at influencing judgment (the definition of propaganda) is too harsh an indictment.

Journalists, like all citizens, are products of their times and cannot divorce themselves from the morals and values of their society. The WW II journalist was no exception. The war revolved around a single over-riding issue—the very survival of civilized societies. Alleged German atrocities fabricated so skillfully by Allied propaganda during WW I, were now reality on a scale beyond the belief and imagination of the most inventive propagandist. Defeat for the Allies would have plunged the world into a new era of the Dark Ages. As Canadian historian Granatstein put it ". . . if the war had been lost, as it so nearly was, the world would

vv

have become a dreadful charnel house of slave peoples controlled by a 'master race'." It was such a possibility that prompted Oxford historian H.R. Trevor-Roper to ask how anyone could have reported objectively on the Nazi Third Reich. War correspondents couldn't and didn't. This emotional commitment to the rightness of the cause did, however, blind reporters to shortcomings in the prosecution of the war, and encouraged a cheerleader style of reporting. Play by play commentary may be a better description. (A significant number of warcos, as they were called, had a sports reporting background, including such famous Americans as Drew Middleton and Canadian Ralph Allen.) Fairly typical of the style at the time was Ross Munro's description of the Canadian raid on Dieppe in *Gauntlet to Overlord.*

> *Now the Germans turned their anti-aircraft guns on us. The bottom of the boat was covered with soldiers. An officer was hit in the head and sprawled over my legs. A naval rating had a gash in his throat and was dying. A few who weren't casualties stood up and fired back at the Germans, even when they knew the attack was a lost cause.*

For homeric prose, it was hard to surpass the CBC's Matthew Halton. Here is part of the late correspondent's report during the battle for Ortona in Italy.

> *. . . soaking wet, in a morass of mud against an enemy fighting harder than he's fought before. The Canadians attack, attack and attack. The enemy is now fighting like the devil to hold us. He brings in more and more guns, more and more troops. The hillsides and farmlands and orchards are a ghastly brew of fire, and our roads four miles behind the forward infantry are under heavy shelling. Not as bad as our own shelling, but bad enough. Sometimes a battlefield looks like a film of a battlefield, but not this. It's too grim. It's a very localized battle with all hell and thousands of troops in a small area. We have fire superiority. We have wonderful soldiers—there's a dogged fierceness about Canadians now—but the enemy is well-disciplined and cunning and he knows all the tricks, clean and unclean. Some of his troops surrender to attacking Canadians. As the Canadian platoon advanced to take the surrender, they were mowed down by flanking machine guns. They were trapped and murdered, just one of the many treacheries. Today we saw one of our stretcher bearers killed by a German sniper.*
> *Listen to the echo of those shells! Those are our guns far behind in such a position that there is this wild echoing.*

Halton was the first broadcast journalist to appreciate the dramatic dimensions background sound gave his radio reports. This was no easy

vv

task in his day. He and his recording engineer crawled to the infantry attack line lugging a bulky spring-winding 78 rpm disc recorder, then kept their fingers crossed hoping the temperamental monster would pick up what Halton called "the sounds of battle." (Although very easy to listen to, his reports were often inaccurate.)

This was unique in North American radio coverage of the war. The American networks didn't allow their reporters to record their reports, or the background sounds. It was a self-imposed rule. Live or nothing. It soon became apparent to American radio reporters that the technology just wasn't there to cover a modern war *live*. (That was to change 50 years later in the Gulf War.) Maybe the trenches of WW I could have been covered that way if home radios had existed, but not a blitzkrieg, which by definition is fast-moving.

Because of this ridiculous situation, ace CBS radio commentator Edward R. Murrow found himself describing in great detail the relentless bombing of London in 1940, without the sound of a single exploding bomb or booming ack-ack gun. He had no choice but to *tell* his listeners what he had heard—"The sound of gunfire has been rolling down these crooked streets like thunder." His colleague William Shirer recalls how "night after night during the worst bombing any city had ever taken there would be a lull just as Murrow went on the air."

Americans depended largely on print reporters like Ernie Pyle to give them a daily blow by blow account of the war. And that was very much how Pyle reported it. He, like most correspondents, ignored the "big picture" to use the parlance of the time, to concentrate on the daily grind of G.I. Joe. Pyle covered the war in microcosm, lionizing the ordinary soldier whether scared to death in a fox hole or in the depths of boredom and melancholy far from home. Pyle's dispatches were written simply, but with flashes of considerable descriptive detail. They were as eagerly awaited in American homes as a letter from a son at the front. Indeed, that is really what his reports were—letters to the folks back home.

> *August 6, 1943—. . . Sicily is really a beautiful country. Up here in the north it is all mountainous and all but the most rugged of the mountains are covered with fields and orchards. Right now everything is dry and burned up, as we so often see our own Midwest in dry summers. They say this is the driest summer in years. Our ceaseless convoys chew up the gravel roads, and the dust becomes suffocating, but in spring time Sicily must look like the Garden of Eden. The land is wonderfully fertile. Sicilians would not have to be poor and starving if they were capable of organizing and using their land to the fullest.*

In another dispatch he displays all the excitement of a twelve-year-old going on his first plane ride—and his readers loved it. Here is part of it.

vv

> _Inside a Super Fortress_
> _In the Marianas Islands, March 1, 1945._
> The B-29 is unquestionably a wonderful airplane. Outside of the
> famous old Douglas DC-3 workhorse. I've never heard pilots so
> unanimous in their praise of the airplane.
> I took my first ride in one the other day. No, I didn't go on a
> mission to Japan. We've been through all that before. I don't
> believe in people going on missions unless they have to. And as
> before, the pilots here all agreed with me.
> But I went along on a little practice bombing trip of an hour and
> a half. The pilot was Major Gerald Robinson, who lives in our
> hut. His wife incidentally lives in Albuquerque, New Mexico, on
> the very same street as our white house.
> I sat on a box between the pilots on the take off and for the
> landing, and as much as I've flown, that was still a thrill. These
> islands are all relatively small, and you're no sooner off the
> ground than you're over water, and that feels funny.

Was this good journalism? Was it journalism at all? It was certainly
what 13 million Americans wanted to read every day. They wanted to see
the war from the ordinary soldier's perspective. With so many of their
"boys" over there, the war was too personal for the average American to
be preoccupied with the so-called big picture. It was the kind of stuff the
milkman in Milwaukee and the housewife in Hoboken could identify
with.

Pyle's reports reflected the unsophisticated country boy he was. They
were at times naive, simple, obvious, even sycophantic. But like the little
boy in Hans Christian Anderson's fable, he knew a naked emperor when
he saw one. This is what he wrote after the American troops landed on a
Japanese-held Pacific island.

> _Men were sleeping on the sand, some of them sleeping forever._
> _Men were floating in the water, but they didn't know they were in_
> _the water, for they were dead._

Both Pyle and Halton became household names in their respective
countries, although as might be expected, the American myth making
machine made a hero out of Pyle far out of proportion to his actual
achievements. When Pyle was killed on a Pacific island in the spring of
1945 by a Japanese sniper's bullet, the nation went into mourning. He
was eulogized by President Truman, politicians, generals, the press and
above all the G.I.s. His life was chronicled on the movie screen, in
libraries, on military installations—even a navy ship was named after
him.

Morley Safer's Canadian modesty may be showing when he suggests
that too much is made of the exploits of war correspondents. Speaking of

his experiences and those of his colleagues in his book *Flashback, On Returning to Vietnam*, he writes, "Correspondents have been elevated to the status of heroes for being mere bystanders. A once- or twice-a-week brush with the war and always a ticket home. We got awards and raises and herograms for telling the occasional truth and questioning a continuing lie. Lucky, arrogant bastards, most of us."

But the nagging question for WW II correspondents and journalists who read their stories today remains: was it pure propaganda and not journalism at all? How much did they cover up? Until someone comes up with a satisfactory definition of journalism there can be no clear cut answer to these questions. Probably the best that can be said is that it was journalism of a particular kind to the virtual exclusion of critical analysis and commentary. Censorship of course played a major, if not *the* major role, in what was filed and what wasn't, as it did during WW I.

Censorship was often self-imposed because responsible correspondents understand the reason for some censorship during wartime. Exposure of military operations to an enemy which might endanger lives is without question a valid reason for the imposition of censorship. The question becomes murkier when incompetence, stupidity and corruption are camouflaged under the "national security" screen. If WW II war correspondents can be faulted for one thing, it was their lack of zeal and enterprise in challenging censorship when it was used to cover up abuses and incompetence in the way the war was being prosecuted.

Operation Tiger is a shocking example. It was the American equivalent of Canada's Dieppe disaster. Six weeks before the D-Day landings on the shores of Normandy in the spring of 1944, the Americans conducted a dress rehearsal on a British beach. A large flotilla of American landing craft loaded with troops, trucks and tanks headed across the English Channel straight for the Cherbourg coast. Seventy miles from the German coastal fortifications, the ships veered sharply portside in a large loop heading back to the English coastline for a beach landing at Slapton Sound. Two warships were to escort the landing craft to protect them against German naval attack. The warships never showed up, but fast German E-boats did. The lumbering landing craft were sitting ducks for the swiftly attacking torpedo boats. In the morning, the bodies of American troops began washing up on the Slapton beach—nearly 800 of them. The survivors were sworn to secrecy under threat of court martial. It took nearly 45 years for the full story to come to light, revealed not by an American, but by an Englishman. It was bungling on a grand and tragic scale but as far as it is known, no one was ever held accountable. It's inconceivable that at least some correspondents didn't know about the fiasco. But the story wasn't reported. Reporters either didn't have the guts

vvv

to defy the military or they failed to see the difference between safeguarding military security and concealing the stupidity of certain military leaders.

On the home front both in the United States and Canada, the press either remained silent or applauded as thousands of west coast citizens of Japanese origin were stripped of their constitutional rights and property and shipped to concentration camps in the interior. Vigilance in tracking down profiteering and shoddy war production was also less than exemplary, although in all fairness not unheard of.

At the beginning of WW II, Canadian Press correspondent Ross Munro learned that a particular model of army truck had a chronic problem of rear axles breaking. Jack Donoghue, with Canadian Army Public Relations during the war, recalls that the military wanted it hushed up. Munro insisted on filing the story with the result that the potentially dangerous problem was rectified.

Even Ernie Pyle, who had the cosiest of relationships with the military, also managed to fire a few broadsides at bungling bureaucracy over the heads of the censors. During *Operation Torch*, the Anglo-American occupation of Algeria, Pyle exposed the military's reluctance to interfere with pro-Nazi local governments installed by the departing Germans. This, despite the fact that local administrations gave Nazi sympathizers free rein to carry out sabotage against British and American forces. His exposé caused a major flap in Congress. Pyle also exposed corruption. The United States was sending shiploads of food but little was showing up in the stalls of the public markets. Algerian housewives blamed the Americans for the shortages while food was being embezzled by profiteers with obvious American military connivance.

Few correspondents bothered with so called "think pieces." Canadian correspondent Lionel Shapiro did. According to Jack Donoghue in his book, *The Edge of War*, Shapiro displayed a talent for "analyzing commanders, their strategy and tactics." Donoghue, Shapiro's conducting officer in northwestern Europe, says he was the first correspondent to report on the disintegration of the unified allied command; of the antagonisms between British Field Marshal Montgomery and the Supreme Commander General Eisenhower. Shapiro also foresaw and warned his readers of the coming cold war which he said was about to tear apart the alliance that fought and won "the ugliest war of all time."

The debacle at Dieppe proved to be the most controversial Canadian operation of the war and Canada's war correspondents didn't escape the controversy. The raid on the heavily fortified French resort town was carried out by a force of 5 000 Canadian troops, several hundred British commandos and a handful of U.S. Rangers. Its purpose was to test Hitler's

vvv

Channel defenses in France and allied seaborne landing techniques and equipment. No doubt some lessons were learned, but from a military viewpoint it was a disaster.

Phillip Knightley, in his book *The First Casualty*, charged that the military not only covered up the Dieppe fiasco, but did so with the connivance of the correspondents who covered it. There is little or no doubt that a military cover-up was attempted. Some correspondents were innocent and in some cases not so innocent dupes in the cover-up.

At least one Canadian radio report was pure fiction. It reported not what happened, but what Allied Command hoped would happen.

> *Dieppe was always a great spot for honeymoon couples, but on the day of this great raid it was a grand spot for Canadian troops and their tanks. For hours, Dieppe was theirs. They held the town, created a great deal of damage there, captured numerous German prisoners and then retreated in perfect order.*

Reports like that must have made even the brass at Combined Operations Headquarters blush and the Germans laugh.

Each of the nine correspondents assigned to Dieppe saw only what was going on in his own small sector of a raid which spanned several miles. While none had a complete picture, most suspected that whatever valuable lessons had been learned, they had been bought at tremendous cost. But in the immediate aftermath of the raid, the truth was that no one knew the whole truth.

The American news services were nevertheless quicker off the mark. The day after the raid, *Associated Press* reported it as a costly operation, but carried no casualty figures.

The cover-up attempt at Combined Operations Headquarters (COH) was doomed to failure from the start. Even under strict war time censorship, the loss of nearly an entire division couldn't be concealed. The Canadian Army knew that, even though Lord Mountbatten's COH did not.

After what Donoghue describes as two weeks of wrangling with Mountbatten's staff, the army was able to release a factual account of what had happened. A few days earlier, a complete casualty list had been issued. Out of 6 000 men, mostly Canadian, 907 were dead, 568 wounded, 2 000 taken prisoner. That constituted three-fifths of the entire force engaged.

The Canadian Army's report written by Colonel C.P. Stacey pinned the blame for bad planning on the British officers at COH but insisted that the raid had taught the military how not to mount the full-scale invasion of Normandy. By war standards, the report was one of optimal candor.

vvv

There is no indication that the blatant attempt at cover-up taught reporters to be more skeptical of future headquarters briefings and to put greater credence on the more candid assessments made by lower ranks in the field. Under most circumstances, the latter should always be part of a correspondent's analytical mix. Statistical statements from the top tend to be politically loaded and self-serving. This is never truer than when generals assume that correspondents are part of their staff.

If Dieppe was questionable, sending Canadian troops to Hong Kong was tragic folly, a fact that largely escaped journalists of the day.

The tiny outpost of the British Empire on the southern coast of China was indefensible. The Japanese, who had massed three divisions 50 km (30) miles away on the Chinese mainland knew it, the British knew it and the Canadian government should have known it.

In a memorandum to his Chief of Staff, Winston Churchill warned that sending more troops was all wrong. "If Japan goes to war there is not the slightest chance of holding Hong Kong or relieving it. It is most unwise to increase the loss we shall suffer there." Indeed, Churchill would have liked to reduce the 12 000 man British force already there to token size, but was afraid such a move would send the wrong signal to the Japanese.

Lord Halifax, Britain's ambassador to Washington, warned both London and Ottawa that sending more men to Hong Kong was absurd. One man who did think the colony could be defended was Major General Ed Grasett, a Canadian serving in the British Army. Not only did he favor sending more troops, he knew exactly where to find them without draining manpower from Britain. The troops would be found in Canada.

Ignoring Churchill's warning, a request based on Grasett's optimism went out to Ottawa for two infantry battalions. The Canadian government snapped to attention and dutifully complied.

In a matter of weeks an expeditionary force of nearly 2 000 men was thrown together. At its core were two activated militia battalions drawn from the Royal Rifles based in Quebec City and the Winnipeg Grenadiers. They were designated as "C Force," which meant not combat ready.

Colonel John Lawson, a former Edmonton school teacher and militia officer, then director of military training in Ottawa told the government the battalions were still far from battle ready. Ottawa silenced Lawson by promoting him to Brigadier and putting him in command of the green troops.

Almost a month to the day after the British request, the ill-fated force sailed from Vancouver unaware that battle-hardened Japanese troops were already preparing to attack Hong Kong's northern defenses. On December 7, hours after the attack on Pearl Harbor, they struck. The

vvv

luckless Canadians, just off the boat, were still waiting for their vehicles and equipment to arrive on another ship.

The butchery that followed during the next 17 days was unprecedented. The Canadians, mostly farm boys and kids from small rural communities, fought as best they could alongside British and Indian regulars.

Many of the Canadians hadn't completed basic training. Some admitted in later years that the only rifle practice they'd had was shooting gophers and firing at tin cans with .22 rifles. One city boy said, "I never fired a shot 'til I got to Hong Kong."

One thing the Canadians were apparently good at was hand-to-hand combat. It wasn't the kind of fighting they chose but it was forced on them when bayonets and courage were all they had left.

In the afternoon of Christmas Day 1941 they surrendered. Of the 2 000 who embarked in Vancouver two months earlier, 557 died in battle or of disease, beatings and bayonetting in prison. Among those killed was Brigadier Lawson. Many of those who returned home after the war died prematurely because of prolonged mistreatment and malnutrition.

And what was the reaction back home? Most Canadians had only the vaguest idea of where Hong Kong was. No Canadian reporters had accompanied the doomed battalions nor was there any criticism in the press of government and military ineptitude. The men, who were so callously sacrificed, were promptly erased from the public consciousness after a royal commission attached no blame to either the government or the military. The papers dutifully echoed the British line, best exemplified by this excerpt from the Cassandra column in the *Daily Mail*: "The defenders of Hong Kong put up a brave show and the Governor (of Hong Kong) takes his place in history. I suppose this loss of life was unavoidable."

The real story of official bungling, stupidity and Japanese atrocities would have to wait until after the war. It was told by Gwen Dew, an American newspaper reporter and the only foreign correspondent on the island when the Japanese attacked. She didn't write the story sooner because like the British, Indian and Canadian defenders, she too became a prisoner of war.

During her career as a journalist, Dew had interviewed a wide range of people, from kings, presidents, movie stars, and sports celebrities to cold blooded killers. But her toughest assignment after her release was to interview the nurses who had been gang raped by Japanese soldiers.

For Dew, covering the fall of Hong Kong was much more than a story. It was a traumatic experience of deep personal dimensions that changed her life for all time.

vv

No account of WW II news coverage would be complete without mention of the military film and photo units. These men were not correspondents in the accepted sense, but their combat footage appeared regularly in the movie newsreels. Without them, today's vast stores of archival film and photos documenting the war would not exist. Armed with little more than cameras, these "soldier journalists" on both sides of the conflict moved with the combat troops and flew with the bomber crews. Unlike civilian photographers and reporters, they had no choice and their efforts weren't always appreciated by their superiors. Captain Frank Duberville of the Canadian Army took the historic pictures of the D-Day landing craft dropping its ramp into the water, revealing assault troops silhouetted against the tower of a railway station, on the beaches of Normandy. They were classic shots taken under fire. When the film arrived in England, his deskbound superiors wanted to know why he had failed to get the names and hometowns of the troops.

Donoghue, from his public relations vantage point in Europe, credited Canadian forces with the fastest combat coverage in every major operation from Sicily, the capture of Rome, the invasion of Normandy to the liberation of Paris. The PR units were made up almost entirely of former civilian reporters and photographers who had a keen appreciation for a scoop.

Casualties among military photographers in all armies were high in relation to the numbers involved. Four Canadian cameramen and two drivers were killed. No civilian Canadian correspondents were killed or wounded, although one was taken prisoner by the Germans. German correspondents, photographers and cameramen, totally integrated into the forces, suffered casualties equal to their infantry.

Given the technology of the day, allied combat coverage was fast, thanks to these conscientious public information units. But that wasn't their main task. Their job was threefold: persuade the press to do stories that boosted morale at the front and at home, maintain military security, and officially document the war in words and pictures. To achieve this, the military had a tendency to view the uniformed press corps as an unofficial arm of their public relations command. In most instances the press acquiesced all too readily, with the result that stories which should have been told, often were not.

U.S. General Dwight D. Eisenhower, the Supreme Allied Commander during WW II, was quite clear on where he thought war correspondents fitted into the picture. He said "I have always considered as quasi-staff officers, correspondents accredited to my headquarters."

After the war, as commanding general of SHAEF (Supreme Headquarters, Allied Expeditionary Force) Eisenhower's attitude towards the press

vv

didn't change. In fact, censorship became stricter than it had been during the war. Three weeks after the German surrender, the *New York Times* protested: "The American people are being deprived of information to which they are entitled . . . It seems almost as though now that there is no enemy to fight, high army officers are spending a large part of their time writing directives to circumscribe the movements and activities of war correspondents."

The American people were indeed being deprived of information they, and the entire world, were entitled to. The biggest and most tragic story of the immediate post war period went largely unreported and remained so for the next 44 years.

It wasn't until 1989, when author James Bacque published his book *Other Losses,* that the world learned of the atrocities committed by the U.S. and French armies against the millions of German prisoners of war taken by the Allies when the Nazi Reich collapsed. According to Bacque's research they were held outdoors in large barbed-wire enclosures. For months they were given little food or water, no shelter and no medical care. Over half a million were turned over to the French as war reparations labour. They were treated so badly that about 250 000 died. Hundreds of thousands more are believed to have perished in the American camps, including women and children. A visit to one camp prompted a French army captain to compare it to Buchenwald. Bacque claims that's exactly what Eisenhower had in mind—giving the Germans back some of their own medicine—because the orders specifying starvation rations, withholding medical supplies and barring the Quakers and the Red Cross from giving aid were all signed "Eisenhower."

Of all the Allied forces which took large numbers of German prisoners, only the British (under some pressure) and the Canadians treated them according to the rules of the Geneva Convention. The Canadians acted under specific instructions from Prime Minister William Lyon Mackenzie King. His attempts to retain the Swiss as neutral observers though were rebuffed by the British, French and Americans.

The British attitude toward POWs and German civilians changed under protest from some influential Britons like publisher Victor Gollancz. Gollancz was an unlikely champion of humane treatment for the defeated Germans. He was a Jew, and was no stranger to German anti-Semitism, not to mention the just revealed horror of the holocaust. Yet, according to Bacque, Gollancz was able to prick the British government's conscience with the words, "I want to feed (Germans) not as a matter of policy but because I am sorry for them . . . If you were to believe our public men, you would think that pity and mercy were positively disgraceful, and that self-interest was a basic ethical duty . . . . "

vv

Gollancz's words had an impact on the British, but failed to move the Americans or the French. Their indifference condemned thousands of men, women and children to death.

Why was the story never reported? Bacque gives a number of reasons: iron-clad military censorship, war hardened anti-German sentiment by the U.S. and French military who thought the Germans had it coming to them, war weary correspondents who were tired of writing about the war and wanted to go home, and lack of interest by editors in postwar Europe. There was also the assumption by a co-opted press that the victorious Allies would treat the vanquished in a firm but fair way, and that the principles on which the war had been waged precluded atrocities prompted by vengeance.

Bacque alleges that to this day the full story is being covered up. Entire files on the subject are missing, and officials involved refuse comment. Publication of his book in the United States has been denied, allegedly because of questionable research methods. This, in spite of corroboration by respected U.S. Army historians, German prisoners of war and American troops on guard duty at the POW camps in question.

Bacque believes responsibility for this black page in postwar history rests with many. The American and French political and military leadership, those French citizens who saw it happening on their soil—and most of all, on a less-than-vigilant free press.

The story surfaced briefly in the French press, along with the disclaimers shifting responsibility onto the Americans. The *New York Times* picked up the story from *Le Figaro*, and carried a mild rewrite along with denials from the American military. Apparently no reporters tried to see for themselves. Drew Middleton, one of America's most illustrious war correspondents, wrote the story for the *New York Times*, based almost entirely on what the military told him. When Bacque interviewed Middleton in 1988 shortly before his death, and told him he'd discovered that as many as half a million German prisoners had died in U.S. camps, the former star war correspondent showed no surprise at that figure, and freely admitted that he had not actually visited the camps, but had merely "driven by."

Bacque's research prompted him to conclude that the press either didn't care or condoned the atrocities. In any event the prejudice of the times prevailed and by design or omission, one of the biggest stories of the war was missed.

Similar scant attention was to be paid 50 years later to Iraq's chemical attack on its own Kurdish population. Five thousand innocent civilians are believed to have died. The Western media, taking their cue from their governments who tilted toward Baghdad in its war with Iran, reported the massacre in routine fashion and promptly forgot about it. It was conveniently revived during the Allied Coalition's war against Saddam Hussein a few years later.

Korean Conflict

Compared with WW II, the Korean conflict in the early fifties was covered in a haphazard way. Canadians were tired of war. Korea presented no epic cause nor a threat to Canadian security. Although fought under the United Nations flag it was essentially an American effort which successfully pushed Soviet supported Chinese and North Korean forces back across the 38th parallel.

Correspondents assigned to the Canadian Special Force, with few exceptions, didn't stay long. Transportation in and out of Korea often depended on the good will of the Americans. A bottle of whisky usually ensured a seat on a military transport. Dress was casual. Civilian clothes interspersed with odd bits of WW II surplus gear were the norm. Coverage was carried out as it had been during WW II under the guidance of military conducting officers, but censorship was lax or non-existent. Basic ground rules were ignored. Names, units, location were all filed in the belief that there was nothing the enemy could do with such information anyway.

Radio reportage was very much in its infancy from both the technical and professional aspects. Recording equipment was still temperamental and bulky. (TV news coverage was a few years away.)

Every radio reporter was determined to emulate Halton in providing listeners back home with the "sounds of battle." At times they got carried away. Many years after the event veteran reporter Larry Henderson (then with private radio) recalled how he had tried to time his foxhole reports to coincide with incoming artillery to catch the full flavor of the war. He did this so regularly that a Toronto columnist suggested that Henderson (later to become the first anchor on CBC-TV National News) must be ensconced somewhere in a Tokyo geisha house, dubbing in background artillery effects.

Larry was one of those rare Canadian journalists with an understanding of international affairs. So, it was natural that when he joined CTV news in the early sixties he took over the foreign editor's desk. He was a good writer, but his ad libs didn't always come out the way he intended. During his assignment with Canadian forces in Cyprus, Larry was doing a "think piece" on the intractable conflict between Turks and Greeks on the island. Somehow, he had discovered a farmer near Nicosia who had grafted four varieties of fruit onto one tree. Seizing on the symbolism, Larry did his TV report standing under the tree. Totally oblivious to the double entendre, his closing words were; "If four fruits can live on one tree, surely the Greeks and Turks can learn to live on one island."

Vietnam

It has been persuasively argued that television in Vietnam changed for all time the way wars will be covered—and perhaps fought. The long-held notion that the media in wartime become a virtual arm of the military, that reporters and troops are brothers in arms, was shattered. There were no Ernie Pyles or Matthew Haltons in Vietnam to glorify the fighting man or promote a great crusade. Both the military and the politicians were perplexed. "Which side are you guys on anyway?" they asked reporters.

Whatever residual trust there may have been between correspondents and the military went up in smoke along with the thatched huts in a Vietnamese village called Cam Ne. For the pro-war faction, Cam Ne became the symbol of press treachery; for the anti-war movement an example of all that stank about the whole war and American involvement in it.

Yet, the incident was filmed with the full knowledge and co-operation of the Marine Corps. CBS correspondent Morley Safer's cameraman simply filmed what happened—marines on a search and destroy mission burning a village suspected of harboring Viet Cong guerillas. It showed marines setting fire to thatched roofs with Zippo lighters and screaming women and children running from their homes. The marines, if they thought of the consequences at all, seemed to feel that somehow the attack would be sanitized and suitably dressed up for the American TV audience. It wasn't. It was shown for what it was—an operation with little or no purpose conceived in haste and carried out with needless brutality.

The Cam Ne incident shocked the world. Nowhere were the reverberations felt more strongly than in the White House, and no one was more surprised by the reaction than Safer himself. In his book *Flashbacks* he writes that it all started out as just another routine field assignment. Even after he returned from the raid, he anticipated no special reaction. But reaction there was. Americans watching the Evening News saw young Americans torching the huts of unarmed peasants. It disturbed them. President Lyndon Johnson didn't like it either, but for different reasons. He saw it as a betrayal of America's valiant fighting men. Bordering on treason. Angrily, the commander-in-chief picked up the phone to lecture the president of CBS: "You just shat on the American Flag!"

Realizing the mess they'd gotten themselves into, the Marine Corps tried to discredit Safer by claiming the Zippo lighter scene had been set up for the cameras, that the interview with the marine in question was full of misleading questions, and so on. It all came to nothing. It's interesting to conjecture how Ernie Pyle would have handled the story.

vv

The government and the military no longer trusted the media. The media lost trust in the authorities. The battle lines became so firmly drawn that it became next to impossible to put anything about the war in proper perspective. The press reported the facts, but just what those facts meant or their significance was in constant dispute. The automatic reaction from the White House, State Department and Pentagon seemed to be wishful thinking at best and outright distortion at worst. The media came to the conclusion that the war, for the Americans, could not be won—that it stank of corruption, profiteering and misguided policies; that the war was commanded by venal South Vietnamese officers and American generals locked in WW II tactics. The military and government view of the media was equally unflattering. They blamed a short-sighted, manipulated, dishonest press for undermining public support for the war. Knowlton Nash, one of CBC's correspondents in Vietnam, concluded that reporters generally gave a more realistic picture of what was going on than the authorities did.

But the media weren't blameless. Results of action were elusive and virtually defied thoughtful analysis. Complicated stories came across as nothing more than another "bang bang" fire fight on TV. There was no time and still less inclination to explain. This was usually not the fault of some very knowledgeable reporters in the field, but of editors back home who demanded pace and action on the evening TV news line up. The same American footage invariably ended up on the Canadian national newscasts. Reporters who tried to cover the political, social and economic ramifications of the war were told by their editors to concentrate on the "real war." The result was that scores of individuals actions were strung together in isolation, giving an extremely distorted picture of what was going on. It was also one-sided.

The massacre of defenceless women and children by a platoon of U.S. infantry at Mai Lai got blanket, although belated, coverage, as it should have. The mass execution of the intelligentsia and prominent citizenry of Hue by the North Vietnamese got cursory treatment. Much of this was due to TV's limitations in news coverage. No pictures, no story. The physical limitations of the small screen added to the distortion.

The Tet offensive launched by the North was a military disaster of such horrendous proportions that for a time Hanoi feared it had lost the war. But the American people were unaware of this. All they saw on their TV screens were dead American boys lying on the lawn of the U.S. Embassy in Saigon. The U.S. and South Vietnam had won an overwhelming military victory but Hanoi had won the psychological battle.

By late 1967, says Knowlton Nash, "the relentless night after night 'bang bang' of Vietnam coverage, along with repeated revelations of

vvv

official lying about what was really happening, created a credibility gap of unbridgeable proportions." The daily military briefings in Saigon became known as "Five o'clock Follies." ·

Paradoxically, all this did not seriously affect the relationship between correspondents and troops in the field. Reporters were sometimes in the way but almost always made welcome. Their presence was a morale booster for young boys lonely and far from home. Like front line troops in every war, they were puzzled about why reporters came. "We have to be here," they would say, "but why in hell do you want to come and have your tail shot at?"

The dangers inherent for correspondents in such a war are reflected in the casualty figures. Forty-five journalists were killed in Vietnam; eighteen reported missing.

Correspondents were also susceptible to psychological strains. The same problem surfaced again a few years later in the jungle warfare of Central America. Getting caught in a crossfire at anytime anywhere was nerve-wracking to say the least. Witnessing atrocities added to the mental strain.

Two years before Saigon eventually fell the Americans had had enough and withdrew. Vietnam, Australian war correspondent Dennis Warner wrote, had been "lost on the pages of the New York Times." Others pointed to the nightly diet of dinner time carnage on the nation's TV screens. William Touey, however, doesn't believe the media were responsible for losing the war through negative reporting. In his book, *Dangerous Company*, he writes, "It was lost, I became convinced, because Americans are an impatient people without a clear and clarion sense of national purpose."

The North Vietnamese recognized this characteristic and used it as part of their psychological strategy to undermine American public support for the war. In the end, public opinion changed because of a dubious cause and all the body bags coming home with no "light at the end of the tunnel."

This view was confirmed 17 years after the American withdrawal by the U.S. Army itself. In a special report, it concluded that faulty government policy, not negative reporting, caused the public to withdraw support for the war.

Army historian William Hammond wrote in his 413 page report that the military withdrawal from Vietnam was triggered by two main factors—rising casualties coupled with a no-win strategy. Hammond found flaws in some news reports, but said the reporting was generally more accurate than the official statements from the government.

But it was, says the report, the casualties, not the news coverage, that turned the tide as it had during the Korean war. "Public support for each

vvv

war dropped inexorably by 15 percentage points whenever the total casualties increased by a factor of 10." The report concluded that even with more positive news reports, the government information officials wouldn't have been able to stop the disintegration of public support.

Falkland Islands

Vietnam did change the way future wars would be reported, but it may not have changed it in the correspondent's favor. Mindful of the lack of "loyalty" shown by the media in Vietnam, Prime Minister Margaret Thatcher was determined not to take any chances when she went to war with Argentina over the Falkland Islands in 1982. The British Navy decided not to take *any* reporters with its task force charged with recapturing the islands. The media were incensed. "How," thundered *The Times*, "can you have a war without us there?" The government relented. An initial number of 10 correspondents and photographers given clearance to board was eventually tripled. Foreign reporters were barred completely and forced to cover the war from the Argentinean side.

Restrictions on British reporters were reminiscent of WW I. In return for letting them go at all, the Thatcher government insisted on "good news." The Royal Navy had other ideas. The task force commander, obviously not skilled in the art of public relations, told reporters flatly that he planned to use them as conduits of misinformation to throw off the enemy. Indeed erroneous information designed to do just that was leaked to the media by senior British officials.

The British authorities, with Vietnam still fresh in their minds, made sure there would be no nightly TV pictures. The military controlled satellite transmission and thus all TV coverage. There was a television blackout. The Argentinean cruiser *General Belgrano* was sent to the bottom with the loss of 250 lives, an Argentinean rocket destroyed HMS *Sheffield*, HMS *Antelope* was sunk, there were bombing raids on the Falklands, but not a single frame of footage appeared on television. By the time the pictures reached TV screens the news was history, prompting one disillusioned reporter to compare the outdated footage to the Dead Sea Scrolls. The papers got little more than bland official photographs. The little copy that got through to London was often censored to the point of being meaningless.

The Americans, Canadians, and other correspondents covering the war from Buenos Aires got out more information than the correspondents with the British Task Force. They also put more stock in statements from the Argentineans than from the British. The British government and military made such a mess of things, that a Parliamentary inquiry was set up after the war to find out why. The handling of the media was particularly disappointing for those correspondents who had dealt with

vv

the highly professional public relations staff of the British Army in Northern Ireland.

Whatever doubts the British military may have had about the way they handled the information side of the Falklands episode, the Reagan administration seemed to think they'd done just fine. In fact, President Reagan did Margaret Thatcher one better. When U.S. forces invaded Grenada the following year, not a single reporter was taken along. Seven years later during the invasion of Panama reporters operated under a restricted pooling arrangement in which a small group of reporters under tight control of the military was allowed to cover the initial stages of an operation and share their information with other reporters.

In all wars, reporters are almost totally dependent on official briefings for the "big picture." And all wars have shown that the military of any nation often deliberately distorts information to hide failure and bungling. It happened again in Panama. American military briefers announced that new stealth fighter bombers had hit Panama's Rio Hato army base. It was learned later, much later, that the planes missed the military target and hit densely populated residential areas inflicting a high death toll, the full extent of which is still not known.

The Gulf War

The Pentagon employed the same secretive policies during the Gulf War—a made-for-television war if there ever was one. The public got lots of pictures, some live, but never the *whole* picture. The American and British military put the media on the shortest leash since WW II. They did so primarily by restricting access and "reviewing" material before it was sent out. As a consequence reporters found that they were often just relaying the information the military wanted released. The picture the public got was therefore impressionistic rather than realistic, and when the military briefers turned off the information taps, the 800 journalists assembled in the Gulf scrambled to find something to say, often resorting to interviewing each other.

Surprisingly, there was little or no protest from the media in the early stages of the buildup to the war. It was a new war being covered by new correspondents. Except for a sprinkling of Vietnam veterans, the press corps was made up of unblooded war correspondents in awe of the high-glitz, high-tech weapons arrayed against the Iraqis. There were questions at official briefings about which defense contractor was coming out on top. (Raytheon, developer of the patriot antimissile missile, was the early winner.)

Reports aired by correspondents in full battle dress were reminiscent of the "cheerleader" prose of WW II. In the words of Marvin Kalb, writing

vv

in the *New York Times*, "there was a certain whiff of jingoism on the airwaves and in print."

CBS's Dan Rather sounded at times more like a Pentagon publicist than a reporter. An interview with an American general was typical. Shaking the general's hand, Rather patronizingly closed his report with the words, "Thank you sir, you're doing a great job."

Even in wartime reporters should strive for some degree of objectivity. It was hard to come by in the Gulf War.

A direct scud hit on a U.S. military barracks at Dhahran days before the war ended was called a "terrorist" attack by NBC's Tom Brokaw. Striking a military target in wartime is not a terrorist act. No matter how tragic, it is an act of war just as surely as allied bombing attacks on Iraqi command centres in Baghdad were legitimate acts of war. It is discouraging to say the least when senior reporters like Brokaw don't know the difference between terrorist acts and acts of war. It is to the Canadian media's credit that they largely avoided falling into "them and us" propaganda traps.

The British press was even more gung ho than the Americans. Their journalists were "loyal." The Iraqi press was "blindly obstinate." The allies laid down "reporting guidelines." The Iraqis "imposed censorship." The Iraqis "kill." The allied side "neutralized." The Iraqis launched "sneak missile attacks." The good guys made "pre-emptive strikes." Their missiles caused "civilian casualties." Ours caused "collateral damage." If the Allied military had written copy for the British and American media they couldn't have done better.

NBC's Arthur Kent, assigned to the Dhahran air base in Saudi Arabia, gave play-by-play commentary on the scud and patriot missile contest as though it were a sporting event. "Yeh, the alarm's gone off—there's the patriot going up after it—a flash—yes a flash—we got it! Looks like we got it!"

The scud reports turned the handsome Calgarian into something of a media star. Kent, like many correspondents struggling for recognition, certainly expected to make a name for himself through his Gulf War coverage. But, he didn't expect to become the war's first heart-throb. The women back home went wild about the tall, dark-haired correspondent. A fan club complete with newsletter sprang up and Arthur Kent buttons and T-shirts sold briskly. To the girls in the NBC newsroom Kent became known as the scud stud.

The scud stud label stuck. Far from resenting the ribbing from friends and fellow reporters, Kent seemed to take a boyish delight in all the attention.

CUMMINGS, *The Winnipeg Free Press*

vvv

"I'm still getting the scud stud stuff," he told me several months after returning from Saudi Arabia, "but it doesn't bother me, it's all in fun. Even my mother got into the act. I was concerned that she might find the whole thing rather undignified—she's 77 you know. Well, my sister got a hold of one of those scud stud buttons with my picture on it from somebody in L.A. and gave it to mum in Calgary. You know what? She wore it to church! The minister probably wasn't amused."

Hours of TV exposure during the war and the celebrity hoopla that followed made Kent an instant star. He still finds it all somewhat overwhelming and he's not at all sure it's his idea of what a foreign correspondent's image should be. "But," he says philosophically, "it'll blow over. Right now I'm so exhausted. It's backbreaking work. Whoever said this is a glamorous business? . . . . I sometimes wonder if it was worth the sacrifices we all had to make, including anchors like Tom Brokaw. . . . Besides," Kent asked me almost plaintively, "how do you follow this story? What do I do next? You know, the war coverage cost the networks a lot of money—millions." Kent went on to say that there was considerable concern at certain network levels over the amount of money spent on war coverage and in a strange twisted way that resentment was subsequently aimed at the reporter who provided the coverage.

After a few weeks of scud watching and second-hand reporting, correspondents began getting restless. People get killed in wars, there are corpses. They wanted to show and write about the reality of war, not the sanitized version the military dished up at the daily media briefings. Reality became not what was happening but what the military cameras were showing us—bridges in the crosshairs suddenly going up in a puff of black smoke. Generals in polished boots and perfectly pressed battle fatigues talking about "degrading" the enemy. (But no pictures of the degradation.)

The military found itself in a bind. Showing dead bodies would fuel the emotions of the growing antiwar movement at home and as Vietnam so convincingly showed, you can't fight a war that way. And, through live satellite transmissions, scud missiles fired into Saudi Arabia and Israel could be seen instantaneously via CNN, not only in Washington but also in Saddam Hussein's Baghdad bunker. Pinpointing impact locations and other details could conceivably have given the Iraqis vital intelligence to readjust their missiles.

The Israelis took elaborate precautions in censoring such information. They disconnected 593 of the telephone calls abroad made by 1 000 foreign journalists who descended on the country to cover the scud attacks, because the stories being phoned out violated Israeli censorship rules. Two American television companies had their international satel-

vvv

lite facilities suspended. One U.S. correspondent had his credentials temporarily lifted.

In every case the reporters had detailed where Iraqi scud missiles were landing. The firing of patriot antimissile missiles, extent of damage and casualties also came under the purview of the Israeli censors.

There were no serious breaches. Indeed the Israeli military was, in the words of Brigadier General Yitzhak Shani, "amazed at how a country like Israel managed to impose censorship to prevent security breaches in this era of sophisticated technology."

Censorship was also unprecedented among the coalition allies. The Pentagon had successfully muzzled the media in Grenada and Panama and was determined to do likewise in the Gulf. Unofficially it adopted retired Marine General Bernard Trainor's dictum of "duty, home, country, and screw the press."[*] Another military officer put it more diplomatically, although the intent of the words was the same; "the spin on the story is more important than the spin on the bomb."

Correspondents who jumped on a chopper and roamed freely for a good story in Vietnam chafed at the restrictions. First-hand reports were limited to Pentagon pools—trips into the field arranged and conducted by the military during which a small number of eligible reporters shared their information with their base-bound colleagues. All material was "reviewed" by military censors before transmission.[**]

Sitting around waiting for scraps of second-hand information wasn't in the grand tradition of the intrepid war correspondent. The military discipline imposed on the reporting ranks didn't break, but there were cracks. The more rebellious began "pool busting," heading toward the battle lines on their own. They were convinced the military restrictions were in place, not because of security, but as one reporter put it, "to cover the military's ass in case of a screw up." The pool busters, or "unilaterals"

---

* General Trainor's unflattering opinion of the media did not prevent him from appearing as a paid expert on network TV newscasts during the Gulf War.

**Censorship during the Gulf War also had its ludicrous moments supplied not by the military but by the BBC, Britain's august state broadcasting institution. Auntie BBC banned the playing of songs that could cause listeners "distress" at sensitive moments during the Gulf conflict. Sixty-seven songs were singled out. Among them were "Walk Like an Egyptian," "Killing Me Softly With His Song" and John Lennon's "Give Peace a Chance."

vvvvvvvvvvvvvvvvvvvvvvvvvvvvvvvvvvvvvvvvvvvvvvvvvvvvvvvvvvvvv
as the military called them, certainly out-hustled the supervised poolers.[*]

The battle for Khafji provided indisputable evidence that pool busting paid off. At Khafji, pool reporters with the 1st U.S. Marine Division weren't allowed to enter the Saudi town until 18 hours after the initial clash with the Iraqi armour. News of the battle in the city therefore came primarily from the renegade reporters operating on their own because the pools couldn't report fully on the liberation of Khafji because, as they didn't see it, they had no detailed information.

British and French camera crews were the first into Khafji to shoot battle scenes well ahead of the American pools. The freely-roving corre-spondents scored other scoops, including the first heart breaking scenes of the huge Iraqi-instigated oil slicks fouling the beaches of the Persian Gulf.

The military took the position that only a carefully supervised pool system could prevent the allied forces from being overwhelmed by reporters and keep reporters themselves from harm's way. The capture of CBS correspondent Bob Simon and his crew by the Iraqis during an unauthorized news scouting trip buttressed the military's position. It did not dampen some correspondents' desire to get a better picture of the war, even if it meant being "captured" by allied forces and returned to their hotel at gunpoint.

Most of the American reporters played by the pool rules until the final days of the war. CBS's Bob McKeown made an unauthorized Patton-like dash for Kuwait City to scoop the world on the liberation.

ABC weakened to allow Forrest Sawyer to hitch a ride with Saudi and Egyptian forces, whose press policies were less rigid than those of the Pentagon. The move paid off for ABC. The network got the first footage of mass desertions from the Iraqi army even before the land war got underway, and Sawyer was the first and only reporter to go along on a bombing mission.

Whether in the long run the military could have maintained its tight control over the media is an open question. The war itself lasted only 42 days, the ground phase only four.

True to tradition established during the Falklands campaign, the British were even more unbending in their "reviews" than the Americans. The French, on the other hand were considerably looser than either the Brits or Americans, allowing their reporters to file totally free of censorship.

---

[*] Unofficial names for correspondents were more colorful. They included *media puke, headache* and *pencil.*

vvv

There was little conflict between the media and the military in the Canadian sector of the Gulf. The Canadians in any event were very much on the fringes of the war. The country's modest contribution to the Allied effort consisted of 5,000 personnel, three warships, two dozen CF-18 jet fighters, one Boeing 707 tanker, support units, and a field hospital committed to British forces. The Canadian military wasn't flooded with correspondents seeking accreditation. Those who did apply were easily accommodated and for the most part given generous access.[*] Apart from basic ground rules concerning units and movements there was little curtailment of coverage until the final days of the war. For some reason never adequately explained, there was a brief news blackout on Canadian fighter aircraft carrying out air to ground missions when reporters were briefly denied access to returning pilots. By the time the blackout was lifted, the war was all but over.

Canadian military officials were, however, not above petty retaliation for what they considered to be negative reporting. *Globe & Mail* reporter Paul Koring was barred from attending a reception for Qatari officials aboard HMCS *Athabaskan*, a Canadian destroyer docked in Qatar. "We're doing this for your own safety," he was told by Commodore Kenneth Summers, Senior Canadian officer in the Middle East. The real reason was that Navy brass was clearly annoyed about an article Koring had written alleging morale problems on board the *Athabaskan*.

As further punishment, Koring was denied access to a news conference called by General John de Chastelain, Canadian Chief of Staff. A military spokesman conceded that de Chastelain barred Koring because "he was offended" by the same morale problem story. On direct orders from Commodore Summers, Koring was also denied co-operation and access at all Canadian Middle East bases. The access restrictions were subsequently lifted, but Koring says he continued to be closely monitored.

But the real rub for Canadian reporters came when they sought access to operations inside Saudi Arabia, where the Americans, British, French and Saudis called the shots. Efforts to get in on allied pools were rebuffed. The CBC's Brian Stewart says, "I tried to play every violin string I could to access the American and British news pools." The traditional close news links between Canada and the United States cut no ice with the Americans. When we asked the British to include us in their pools, Stewart says, "they laughed in our faces."

---

[*] Courtney Tower, Ottawa editor of *Readers' Digest*, was the only Canadian reporter allowed to fly on a mission during the Gulf War.

vvv

The Canadians then turned to the Saudis, and persuaded them to form an international pool composed of 32 nations rotating around 15 positions. But again the Canadians got short-changed. Although Canada was the fourth largest contributor among the non-Arab coalition members, it was given only one spot in the pool. Tiny Monaco[*] by contrast got four. Austria, which sent no military aid to Saudi Arabia, was given two positions, as were Brazil and Portugal.

Why were Canadian correspondents subjected to that kind of treatment? "Simple," says Stewart, "our government didn't lobby for us, the way other countries did for their correspondents."

Once the ground phase of the war was launched it went so well for the U.S.-led coalition forces that restrictions were rapidly loosened. Uniformed reporter teams moved so freely that Iraqi soldiers were surrendering to them. The ground war had not yet begun when a *Life* photo unit was flabbergasted to run into four fully-armed Iraqi soldiers who wanted to surrender to them. They were so flustered in fact that as they were heading back to Dhahran with their quarry, they suddenly realized they hadn't taken any pictures. They brought their vehicle to a skidding halt, ordered the Iraqis out and reenacted the event for their cameras.

The Gulf War, like all wars, claimed silent casualties. CNN's Bernard Shaw returned home after witnessing the first aerial assault on Baghdad which he said "felt like being in the centre of hell," to find a very stressed-out family. "I know what my wife was going through," he told other reporters. "Now that I've seen the after effects I've decided I'll never put her and my children through that experience again."

Shaw says in 27 years of reporting he's never turned down an assignment, but insists he will if he thinks there is imminent danger and pain for his family.

Peter Arnett, Shaw's colleague in Baghdad, was free of family ties and stayed on in the Iraqi capital to man the CNN bureau. He was, for some time, the only American to be allowed to stay.

One of a number of no-brand-name reporters in CNN's stable of newsmen, Arnett became an overnight household name around the world although he was already something of an institution within the news business itself. He had received the highest accolade possible from his peers, "a correspondent's correspondent."

---

[*] There may have been some justification for this. Radio Monte Carlo is listened to widely in the Middle East.

vv

A 30-year veteran of international reporting, the 56-year-old New Zealander won the Pulitzer Prize for his work during the Vietnam war as an AP correspondent. He stayed in Vietnam for the entire war—13 years on the front lines.

So it was not surprising that he volunteered to stay on in his office in Baghdad's Al Rashid Hotel after his colleagues left, to witness the devastation rained on the Iraqi capital first-hand. With typical insouciance he commented, "I've been in much more dangerous situations in my career with much less attention than I'm getting now. It's just another story." Arnett was under no illusions about the restrictions he'd be obliged to work under, or that he would at times be manipulated by his Iraqi hosts. His rationale was that some news is better than no news and that there was a pressing need for an impartial witness to report objectively after the event.

Few would argue that it was the right decision. It was useful to have a window on events even if it was murky and small. Truth in war is hard to come by at the best of times. It can take days, months, even years to know. History needs reporters like Peter Arnett.

His efforts weren't appreciated by all. Senator Alan Simpson of Wyoming branded him a traitor and a Hussein mouthpiece even though his dispatches were clearly labelled as censored by the Iraqi military. That wasn't good enough for Senator Simpson and many other Americans, including some journalists. They thought Western reporters had no business even trying to report the war from the enemy's camp, that anything they were able to say would color the war in Iraq's favor. A convincing case can be made that Arnett's reports should have been put into some sort of context by CNN, not simply labelled.

Nevertheless, CNN certainly remained Washington's eyes and ears in Baghdad and the only link between the two warring capitals. When 14 bomb- weary foreign correspondents who had been authorized to work in Iraq wanted to leave for Jordan, it was Arnett who alerted CNN headquarters in Atlanta on the number of cars, colors and travel time. The information was relayed to the American military to ensure the convoy wouldn't be attacked by Allied aircraft.

The Gulf War presented journalists with a classic ethical conflict. Is it possible to cover a war involving "your" side objectively? Can a reporter avoid becoming emotionally involved when his or her country's young men and women are engaged in life and death combat?

The answers to these questions are not easy to come by, but there are answers. To begin with, reporters whose country is at war should neither pretend to be neutral on the one hand nor act as cheerleaders on the other. The kind of cheerleading the Americans got from some of their senior

vvv

correspondents like Rather wasn't professional. It cheapened coverage. It is even unnecessary, indeed undesirable to refer to your country's side in a conflict as "we." The true journalist does not allow his or her feelings to get in the way of dispassionate reporting.

In a conflict where the likes of Saddam Hussein are inflicting unspeakable atrocities on their own people and those of neighbors, it is not only impossible, but dishonest to pretend to be totally objective. In such cases the correspondent is obliged to walk a fine line between being a responsible citizen as well as a good journalist.

It is imperative never to assume that your government is always telling the truth nor that the enemy is always lying. Every effort has to be made to verify what both sides are saying. Given the restrictions imposed during the Gulf War that's not easy. Nor will it get easier. With their quick win, the Allies will almost certainly try to repeat their "successful" media policy. (As the British did after the Falklands War and the Americans after Grenada and Panama.)

The use by TV networks of retired generals and other high-ranking ex-officers as specialist analysts is one leak in the system now being scrutinized by Western defence departments.* These people have had training and gained expertise in military tactics and strategy. To stand in front of a map, diagram or sandbox and analyze various military options available for all the world to see, including your country's enemy, is a moral question the media must address. The Allied commander in the gulf, General Norman Schwartzkopf, had his own word for the use of military experts. "Disgusting." The practice may very well be the next target for the censors.

But the cards aren't entirely stacked against the reporters. In any war the military needs the media as much as the media need the military. No army can successfully fight a conflict, especially a protracted one, without public support, and that support is sustained or destroyed in the newsrooms of the nation.

The Gulf War showed that somehow the military and the media must reestablish an atmosphere of trust and responsibility. To end the current gridlock in military media relations, correspondents must convince the generals that they *can* be trusted to report responsibly without endangering soldiers' lives or sabotaging military operations. The military, on the other hand, must realize that it is a short-sighted policy to shield the public

---

* These retired military officers appearing as analysts on the American networks were paid an average of $1 500 per day.

vv

from the unpleasant realities of modern warfare and to allow the heroic efforts of the troops themselves to go unrecorded.

History too is cheated. Except for highly restricted archival footage shot by the military itself, there is no record of the actual fighting that went on in history's most extraordinary war, in which several hundred died on one side, and perhaps as many as 100 thousand on the other.[*]

Despite all the roadblocks and pooling restrictions, TV crews did manage to shoot some spectacular and dramatic footage. Often they faced the reporter's ultimate frustration, getting a good story and not being able to get it out. In this age of electronic wizardry, the Gulf War reporter often discovered to his dismay that no satellite time was available to transmit a hot story. With nearly a thousand reporters supplying saturation coverage (of what was available) the satellite system was being strained to capacity.

The war coverage created more demand for "birds" in orbit than were up there. The European Satellite consortium, *Eutelsat*, saw its traffic double after the first Iraqi scud landed in Israel. Washington-based *Intelstat's* bookings nearly tripled during the war as did U.S. *Comsat's*. *Comsat's* daily bookings doubled over the previous peak recorded during another hot news story, the massacre in China's Tiananmen Square crackdown. The correspondent's dilemma during the Gulf War was further exacerbated when Iraq's uplinks were cut off because Baghdad hadn't paid its *Comsat* bills. TV networks are now using their own smaller mobile uplinks, operating from trucks which can be set up in about six hours.

But the modern war correspondent's biggest challenge is not a technological one. It is a basic problem that hasn't changed since Russell travelled pad and pencil in hand to the Crimea. The issue revolves around access, censorship and the freedom to responsibly report the facts and the truth as the correspondent sees them.

The question the media are asking themselves in the aftermath of the Gulf War is whether the war correspondent is dead—killed by political and military expediency. Were security and "family consid-erations" cited to justify news blackouts as convenient excuses to shield the public from the horrible realities of war? To prevent an erosion of public support? "Trees are falling in the forest," wrote American columnist Rheta Grimsley-Johnson, "but making no

---

[*] There is disagreement over how many Iraqis died. The Pentagon is sticking to its original estimate of 100 000. The British estimate comes in much lower at 30 000 dead.

vv

erosion of public support? "Trees are falling in the forest," wrote American columnist Rheta Grimsley-Johnson, "but making no sound." The war seemed to prove to Western democracies what they are still unwilling to concede publicly; if the media are given free rein to cover armed conflict, war becomes an untenable instrument of foreign policy. War, it seems, cannot be successfully waged under the glare of TV lights. Nor can it be successfully covered that way. The media, television in particular, became enmeshed in their own technology. Visual thrills replaced thought. Facts meant what the military briefers said they meant.

Victor Hugo once said that there are three kinds of audiences: those who demand thoughtful content, those who demand passion and the mob which demands action. In the Gulf War, the media and the military catered shamelessly to the latter.

Living   Dangerously

. . . You'll meet a lot of interesting people when you go to Ishmaelia.

"Mightn't it be rather dangerous?"

Mr. Slater smiled; to him it was as though an Arctic explorer had expressed fear that the weather might turn cold.

— Scoop, by Evelyn Waugh

JOURNALISM HAS BEEN DESCRIBED AS THE WORLD'S most dangerous profession, based on the number of casualties in relation to the number of practitioners. Some might dispute that statement, but no one can deny that the casualty toll is high and growing.

In a 10-year period between 1970-80, 154 journalists were killed or disappeared in Latin America alone. And during those years, 21 journalists, mostly foreign correspondents, were left dead in the jungles of Cambodia. In 1989, according to the Paris-based *Press Watch Organization*, 65 journalists were killed or died in detention. Two hundred and forty were arrested and detained during that year. In Sri Lanka five journalists were killed in one 12-month period starting in the fall of 1988. In 1990, 23 journalists died while doing their job. Many more left the profession because of death threats from violent nationalist organizations. By 1991, the death toll had climbed dramatically to 84, the highest annual toll on record.

Insurance rates tell the story most eloquently. In the late eighties, coverage for one American or Canadian reporter on a dangerous assignment cost upwards of $10 000 per month. For a TV crew, the cost could run well over $30 000. Those figures are escalating every year.

Danger has always been an inseparable part of the profession. As long ago as 1830, George Borrow, author of *Bible in Spain*, found it hard to believe the danger and deprivation English correspondents were willing to endure for the sake of a story. Describing coverage of the interminable Carlist wars, he wrote, "The activity and energy they display are truly remarkable . . . While in Spain they accompanied the Carlist and Christino Guerillas on some of their most desperate expeditions, sleeping on the ground, exposing themselves fearlessly to hostile bullets, to the inclemency of the winter and the fierce rays of the summer's burning sun."

This kind of apparent fearlessness was observed again a hundred years later. But this time it was called folly.

vvv

Gordon Sinclair, reporting on the Japanese invasion of Manchuria in 1937 for the *Toronto Star*, wrote that Japanese reporters had a higher casualty rate than the soldiers. The situation was unusual in that reporters took unconscionable risks by going out of their way to find the most dangerous action. He described the reporters' folly in typical Sinclair prose: "brave men die with their boots on, for a pittance and never dream they're suckers."

The question correspondents constantly ask themselves is "when to risk and when not to risk?" No satisfactory answer to that question has yet been found. Some news organizations give their reporters a set of guidelines to follow. Most do not. *The British Broadcasting Corporation* is one of those that provides no formal guidelines. Instead, the BBC relies on the common sense of the correspondent on the ground. The BBC however, like *Agence France Presse* (AFP), will not send an inexperienced journalist on a dangerous assignment. While the BBC demands a minimum of two years service in their news organization before a reporter is sent anywhere dangerous, AFP insists on no less than 10 years experience with their own organization.

It is nearly impossible to draw an accurate profile of a responsible foreign correspondent. Recklessness is not a desired trait, but neither is extreme caution. Michael St. Pol, AFP's director of International Affairs, worries that "too much emphasis on caution, or conservative coverage slips into self-censorship." And, self-censorship in reportage can lead to distortion at best and dishonesty at worst.

In his book *Words of War*, veteran Canadian correspondent Jack Cahill recounts an incident in Saigon involving a TV crew from Radio-Canada that seems to illustrate St. Pol's concern of being overcautious. Cahill tells of the Montreal-based crew flying into the South Vietnamese capital in the last agonizing days before its fall. They seemed surprised that a real war with actual bombs and bullets was raging on the outskirts of the city.

"It doesn't seem civilized here" the correspondent remarked after Cahill gave him an overall briefing. He and his crew stayed two days, interviewed the archbishop of Saigon and hastily flew back home.

The *Deutsche Press-Agentur* and British *Reuters News Agency* both have set guidelines for their correspondents in the field. Like the BBC and *Agence France Presse* and the North American agencies, both stress experience, but give their correspondents wide latitude in deciding whether or not to move into a danger zone and when to leave.

In a clear recognition of the heightened dangers faced by TV crews and photographers, *Reuters* instructs its reporters to try to avoid travelling with them, and when this is unavoidable, not to stand or sit too close. It

vv

is small wonder that the cameramen, TV crews and photographers are still considered journalistic heroes in the business.

Also to be avoided, according to *Reuters* guidelines, is travelling in jeeps and semi-military vehicles unless with an army patrol. Wearing military uniforms is usually out, unless the reporter is accredited to a particular military group.

With typical attention to Teutonic thoroughness, the DPA guidelines place considerable emphasis on such details as expert preassignment briefings, library research, language fluency and special life, health and accident insurance plans. And, a final stern warning from DPA management—no involvement in any way in espionage and secret service contacts.

News organizations providing no formal guidelines (the vast majority) do so for specific reasons. In the words of one representative, "(We) depend on correspondents using common sense and their own instincts in difficult situations . . . we don't think such skills can be taught."

Reporters generally, and foreign correspondents in particular, accept the reality that taking risks is part of their job. Invariably though, the question is, how much risk for what kind of story? Is it worth dashing across a street exposed to gunfire to get another sound bite for a radio report? Obviously not. Some stories are worth more risk than others and no two situations are exactly alike.

Norwegian correspondent Per Egil Hegge, who has been in his share of tight spots, doubts whether any sensible advice can be given beyond the obvious: "Have a good grasp of the situation you face, keep your composure and above all, don't try any heroics." The following incident, jotted down in my notes during the Vietnam War, tragically illustrates this point.

On the first day of the Cholon offensive in Saigon during the Vietnam war, five recently-arrived correspondents jumped into an open vehicle and headed for the action. They kept going up an alley even though they saw residents fleeing in the opposite direction. They came to a road block manned by the Viet Cong. The young journalists called out, "bao chi, bao chi" (journalist in Vietnamese). The V.C. officer in charge levelled his pistol and shot one reporter in the head at point blank range. The V.C. around him opened up with automatic fire, instantly killing three more. The fifth dropped to the ground and played dead. When the shooting stopped, he jumped up and literally ran for his life, escaping up a narrow alley.

This was a clear case of misguided heroism of young journalists in a war zone trying to be macho. The survivor admitted to a sense of fear and

vv

foreboding as they entered the area but did not want to be the first to chicken out.

The tragic incident brings to mind the words of Starbuck in *Moby Dick*: "I shall have no man in my boat who is not afraid of the whale." It also illustrates the classic dilemma of "unblooded" correspondents who are sent to dangerous areas already well-mined by their predecessors. Anxious to make their mark with editors and get a new angle on a story, they are tempted to get much closer to the action than is prudent. Experienced people of course also fall into this trap.

Michael Laurent could be described as both fearless and foolhardy. On the eve of the fall of Saigon the French photographer was getting dramatic shots with a telephoto lens of North Vietnamese troops advancing through heavy foliage toward Saigon. Seemingly oblivious to danger, he continued looking for that one shot at closer range that would capture the moment. The advancing soldiers spotted the Pulitzer Prize-winning photographer, opened up with automatic fire and killed him instantly.

What explains the taking of such unconscionable risks? There is no single answer. Combat photojournalists are, almost without exception, restless, tortured souls constantly in search of an adrenal rush. There is always something to prove to the editors back home, to other photographers, and perhaps most importantly, to themselves.

American camerawoman Linda Olszenewski wasn't prepared for the risks some of her colleagues took during the Afghanistan war. After one of them was killed by a Soviet helicopter gunship she told a BBC interviewer, "They were gutsy to the extreme. It's so competitive out there. They push each other closer and closer to the action. You gotta get close—you gotta get that shot. Bombs going off all around you but you gotta get that shot. It was crazy."

The drive to capture life and death images for posterity at all costs becomes a form of madness. Naoko Nanjo left her comfortable but boring middle class life in Yokohama to become Japan's leading photojournalist in Afghanistan. She also became one of ten journalists to die in that war. Practically torn to shreds by shrapnel, her last request to a fellow cameraman was, "Please take my picture."

Afghanistan was a war that seemed to drag on forever, from 1979-88. Perhaps for that reason it was covered almost entirely by free-lancers for the mainstream media whose interest in coverage waxed and waned in direct proportion to the action footage available.

To get the kind of pictures that were saleable these free-lancers, especially the photojournalists and cameramen, took high risks and endured unbelievable hardships. Like most inexperienced journalists, they were out to make a name for themselves.

vvv

They seemed to believe, even more so than the veteran journalists, that as observers they were above the battle, immune to the bullets flying all around.

The fatalists among them trotted out the tired cliché that if a bullet had their name on it, there wasn't much they could do about it. The late Neil Davis, a veteran combat cameraman, was closest to the truth when he used to say that he wasn't all that concerned about the bullet with his name on it, it was the one labelled "to whom it may concern" that worried him.

Danger indeed often arises out of the trivial, the perfectly ordinary, the unexpected, like standing too close to an intended target or a case of mistaken identity. The following entries from diary notes illustrate the point.

August 13/71—Belfast

An early day of shooting to pick up footage around Belfast turned into a harrowing experience. Intrigued by churches stranded in wrong neighborhoods. We shot boarded up Protestant church in Catholic area. Found closed Catholic church on Protestant turf. In court yard, beautiful white marble statue of Madonna and child protected by rolls of barbed wire with British soldier standing guard.

Terrific symbolic shot. Decide to interview soldier. Phil Pendry just gets camera rolling. There's a hail-like clatter on sidewalk. Soldier dives for cover. Orders me and crew to do same. Sounded like someone dropping marbles on concrete. Soldier yells that it is gunfire apparently coming from building on other side of a vacant recently bulldozed lot. Everybody grabs a piece of film equipment and crawls belly to the ground through the barbed wire back to the church. Emerge in backyard of a funeral home where caskets being unloaded. Always amazed more reporters aren't killed or hurt in this hate-filled place.

August 18-19/71—Belfast

Sunday morning. Still shaky. Feels like a block of ice lodged in my gut. Guess I came close to 'buying the farm' last night. At least that's what McNally tells me. Started out as a routing filming of Catholic pub in Lower Falls on a Saturday night. McNally's band plays in the place, so filmed there at his suggestion. Said he had good connections with IRA types who hang out there.

Producer Martyn Burke and Pendry were shooting band on stage. I sat down in far corner to observe and take notes. Three tough looking guys sat down two tables away staring at me rather menacingly, I thought. Suddenly all tables clear—everybody's on the dance floor except me and the newly-arrived patrons. Just as

vv

suddenly McNally dropped his guitar and dashed over to the trio of toughs. Whispered in the ear of one, all the while glancing nervously my way. They left and McNally advised me to grab a table near the stage.

At closing time, McNally quickly ushered us out the back way. Told me the three were IRA gunmen who thought I looked suspiciously British. How stupid of me. Wearing a navy blue blazer was bad enough. What the hell was I thinking when I added my old regimental ascot?

August 23/71—Belfast

We did another stupid thing today. Nearly got shot up by a British Army patrol. Pendry decided best way to get running street shots was to set up camera with long lens on tripod in back of John Jourdan's English-style taxi. Got in about three minutes of shooting before two British Army vehicles boxed us in, machine guns trained on taxi. Soldiers, guns drawn, check inside of cab. We explained what we were doing. Sergeant red with anger, chewed us out. "You silly bastards, how are we to know that's a camera and not a gun. You chaps bloody well nearly got it, you know."

In today's vast arsenal of conventional weapons, no weapon is more deadly than old-fashioned artillery. It is also the most difficult to defend against. It's unfortunate that few correspondents assigned to combat zones bother to even learn the basics of commonly used weapons, especially the firing patterns, bursting distances, range of artillery shells and the use of structure and ground shelter. Flak jackets and bullet-proof vests are often shunned as too cumbersome. Inexperienced combat reporters also have difficulty in comprehending the damage those jagged projectiles of hot metal called shrapnel can inflict on the human body. It was artillery that got CTV's Clarke Todd in Lebanon.

In 1983, the Israelis pulled out of the Shouf mountains overlooking Beirut. The area was prime strategic real estate contested by both the Druse and Christian militias. A battle was an absolute certainty. When Todd arrived from his London base, the hills were already a near no-man's land. He correctly predicted that the village of Kfar Mata would be the centre of the action. The villagers apparently knew it too, because by the time Todd got there the town was nearly deserted. And it was at Kfar Mata during one of the first artillery salvos that shrapnel tore into Todd's chest. The other reporters and camera crews on the scene fled for their lives. Todd, mortally wounded, was left to die in an abandoned shell-pocked house.

Catching a stray bullet is one of the combat reporter's biggest worries. That's what happened in Iran to my Bonn colleague Joe Alex Morris of

vvv

the *Los Angeles Times*. As the demonstrations against the Shah's forces were mounting in intensity in the late seventies, a group of reporters found themselves on "the wrong side of the fence" with a group of demonstrating students. Government forces opened fire, forcing a group of reporters to take refuge in a store. They went up one floor for a better look. When the building was sprayed with bullets everyone hit the floor. Morris was first up, to see what was happening. At that precise moment, a bullet smashed through the closed blind killing him instantly.

Even the most experienced, battle-hardened correspondent must be constantly on guard against complacency. As has been mentioned, the ordinary, the routine, even the mundane often spring the biggest surprise.

Neil Davis, an Australian-born cameraman-correspondent based in Bangkok for NBC was experienced and street smart. He had done outstanding work in Vietnam and Cambodia for Visnews, the CBC and NBC. He had covered wars and upheavals in Sudan, Lebanon, The Philippines, Zaire, Angola, Uganda, Zimbabwe, Iran and Iraq. Jack Cahill, who knew him well, described Davis as a "correspondent's correspondent." He constantly weighed the value of the story against the risk. Yet the assignment that took his life was a two-bit story that wouldn't have merited more than a few seconds on the evening news.

On September 9, 1985, Davis interrupted an evening of socializing at the Bangkok Foreign Press Club to check out a tip about an attempted coup in the Thai capital. It was a tin pot coup attempt. A handful of disgruntled army officers with a few tanks, trained cannon and machine gun fire on a radio station. Davis and his American sound man, Bill Latch, were pinned down in a crossfire between the tanks and the loyalist machine gunners in the radio station. A lull in the shooting was short-lived. As they crouched low and continued to roll film, two shells exploded against a wall behind Davis and Latch. Shrapnel ripped into both of them, leaving them mortally wounded. Davis died within seconds while keeping his camera rolling—in effect, recording his own death.

Nowhere is the cardinal rule of never arguing with anyone carrying a gun or in command of those who do more important than at roadblocks and checkpoints. Often they are manned by kids toting AK-47s. Whether they are manned by government forces or insurgents, they can be dangerous and unpredictable. They can amount to nothing more than a short stop for identification, a friendly warning and wave-on, or they can be sudden death traps.

No matter how much pressure there is to get the story, in such circumstances it is imperative for correspondents to keep their composure and not do anything that could be interpreted as provocation by an armed

vvv

individual in authority whether in uniform or not. In any confrontation of this kind, the odds are decidedly not in the reporter's favor.

On June 20, 1979, ABC correspondent Bill Stewart's small van stopped on a side road of a highway near Managua, Nicaragua. Stewart got out to check on a road block on the highway manned by President Anastasio Somoza's National Guard.

No one knows how the conversation went between Stewart and the soldiers. Shielded behind some trees, the crew in the van filmed the horror that was to follow.

Stewart was forced to lie face down on the ground. A guardsman then calmly walked up to him and shot him through the back of the head. He died instantly. His Nicaraguan interpreter was also executed.

The horrified crew sped off toward downtown Managua. Response from the authorities was lethargic. The crew was determined to get the tape past government censors and out to New York, which was no mean task. The television station was owned by the Somoza family. A censor with his finger on the button screened all the pictures leaving the country via satellite. The crew decided to shoot reams of boring, inconsequential footage. That footage was put on one machine, the crucial Stewart tape on another. They rolled the useless material—street scenes, buildings, trees, parks. The censor's eyes glazed. Once distracted, the tape operator punched up the Stewart tape. By the time the censor realized what was going on, the incriminating pictures were in New York. The evening newscasts showed the shocking scene: Stewart being forced to lie face down on the ground—the guardsman pointing his American-made weapon at Stewart's head—the shot and Stewart's body levitating, then slumping motionless.

Peter Worthington recalls being in the company of the late CBC correspondent Norman Depoe during the Biafran War. Depoe, who was a brilliant, hard-drinking reporter with a somewhat short fuse, got into a shouting match with one Colonel Benjamin Adekunle over permission to travel in the war zone. As Worthington tells it, the flamboyant Nigerian war hero Adekunle, known to his fans as the Black Scorpion, dispensed a bit of venom himself. He forced Depoe to stand on the Port Harcourt airport runway unprotected from the scorching African sun without food or water. At nightfall he was packed on the evening flight to Lagos "dehydrated, deflated and disconcerted."

The German philosopher Nietzsche suggested that the state tends to take on a character and personality of its own, and once created acts quite independently of its creators. Much the same can be said about a mob, a Frankenstein's monster in frightening form. People, who as individuals

vv

are quite rational and sane, become a seething mass of humanity out for blood—anyone's.

Working out of Cairo during the Six Day War, correspondents Worthington, then of the *Toronto Telegram*, Don McGillivray of *Southam News* and Gunnar Nielson, a Swedish reporter, found themselves in the middle of just such a life-and-death situation.

In his book, *Looking for Trouble, a journalist's life and then some*, Worthington relates how a simple trip to the main railway station took an ugly and menacing turn. The following is the gist of Worthington's account.

There were wild rumors that 3 500 Israeli prisoners were due to arrive in the Egyptian capital. They were skeptical, but the taxi drivers swore the rumors were true. The three newsmen grabbed a cab to check it out. The gathering crowd had grown so large, the taxi driver parked his cab on the fringe and lead the reporters toward the railway station. The closer they got, the heavier the crush of people, all anxious to catch a glimpse of the Israeli prisoners. There was a holiday atmosphere on the outer edge of the human mass, but as the three got to the high iron fence surrounding the station, the mob pressing against it were shouting anti-Israeli slogans and impatiently demanding to see the prisoners. The farther they went, the uglier the mob got. There were shouts of "bring out the Jews."

Once at the main gate, soldiers quickly let the correspondents into the station area, but were immediately told to leave. There were no Israeli prisoners.

"It is a mistake," a young police colonel told them. "A rumor. You know Cairo."

The colonel was adamant. No, the reporters could not stay in the railway station. "No one invited you here," the colonel continued. "You came on your own, leave on your own. And I would hurry if I were you."

McGillivray and Nielson plunged into the crowd. Worthington hesitated. To go into that maelstrom was the height of foolishness, yet it was even more foolish to be separated from his companions. He dove in after them and was immediately encircled by the waving, screaming, spitting mob. Those immediately around the correspondents knew they weren't Israeli prisoners but those farther back did not. Soon a chant went up that they were the Israeli prisoners. Some people started throwing punches at the three foreigners who now had visions of being torn apart by the raging mob.

As things began to get even uglier, a young Egyptian attached himself to the hapless reporters. He shouted to the crowd to leave the men alone, that they were journalists and not Jewish prisoners. The mob would have none of it. The good Samaritan was punched and kicked for his efforts.

vv

Then an older man came to the reporters' defense, but he too provoked nothing but abuse and shouts of "Jew lover."

Eventually they reached the fringe of the crowd, where to their amazement stood a parked taxi—its driver blissfully asleep at the wheel. They pushed into the cab with the crowd closing in around the vehicle, rocking it and pounding the roof as the driver casually drove off with the three reporters.

The British press played up the story but the editors of Worthington's own paper back in Toronto seemed slightly bored by the whole episode and gave it modest play. After all, it was just another escapade of derring-do their hero had gotten himself into again. But Worthington knew just how close the call had been, summing it up this way: " . . . I think the three of us were just an incident away from becoming statistics of the Six Day War."

As combat coverage goes, the 1973 Arab-Israeli war took the prize for incongruity. Correspondents commuted to the battle fronts from luxury hotels in Tel Aviv and Jerusalem because Israeli forces refused to allow foreign reporters to overnight with the troops. Some correspondents made the trip in rented cars, others took the military bus that shuttled them daily between hotel and front.

It was, however, anything but a regular 9 to 5 job. The hours were long. A round trip took 10 hours to the Sinai and over 5 hours to the Golan Heights. The hotel staff would prepare boxed lunches the night before. The day invariably ended with the official war briefing at the defense ministry in Tel Aviv where censored stories would be filed. By then restaurants would be closed, but there was still time to unwind and swap stories at the bar. Early the next morning it was off to the front again.

The casual routine masked the very real dangers the front-line correspondents faced each day. At times there were no military police along the Damascus highway, resulting in reporters overshooting Israeli advance elements and driving precariously close to Syrian lines.

Choosing the right-colored car posed a dilemma. Olive green or khaki-colored vehicles could be mistaken for military staff cars by the other side. Some correspondents thought brightly painted cars that were obviously civilian provided the best protection. That theory was demolished one day when Nicholas Tomalin of the *London Sunday Times* stopped near the front to let his photographer take pictures of gutted tanks. His red car caught the eye of a Syrian antitank gunner. A direct hit from a wire-guided missile killed Tomalin instantly.

The pitfalls for foreign correspondents in the Arab Middle East seem endless. Something as innocent as the sound of your name can land you

vvv

in trouble. Authorities are constantly on the lookout for people they consider Jewish interlopers.

American correspondent William Touey relates such an incident in his book *Dangerous Company*. A Jewish colleague applying for a visa is asked by an Arab airport immigration officer whether Hochstetter is a Jewish name. Since it is a name of German origin the reporter quickly replied, "Not necessarily." He got his visa.

A problem of similar nature appears in my diary.

> *May 16/77—Baghdad*
> Arrived in Iraqi capital today. Arrival coincided with that of a Canadian communist delegation here for the 35th anniversary of Iraq's governing Baath Socialist Party. I accidentally got the red carpet treatment. Literally. Ushered into the VIP lounge for sweets and coffee followed by limo service to luxury hotel. Desk couldn't find my reservation. Mistake discovered. I was booked into the Ali Baba Hotel—definitely not luxury.
>
> Airport customs and immigration was just a quick formality, but ran into a bit of a hassle at check in counter at the Ali Baba. When asked for my passport and visa, clerk asked if I was Jewish. I said no. Then wanted to know if I wasn't Jewish, why my first name was Abram. An explanation that my Mennonite parents had a predilection for Old Testament names seemed to satisfy him, but he insisted on keeping my passport for a further check.
>
> Hope I don't get caught up in a hostage or highjacking incident and have to go through this explanation again. The guy with the AK-47 might not believe me or bother to check it out.
>
> *May 17/77—Baghdad*
> Made the evening TV news in Baghdad tonight. There was a shot of me descending the ramp of an Iraqi jet liner, greeted by government officials on a red carpet. The only part of the Arabic report I could understand was "Communist delegation from Canada." So, that was why I'd gotten the VIP treatment—they thought I was part of the Canadian Communist Party delegation!

For all their dangers, the Middle East wars paled in comparison to the risks inherent to covering the civil war in Cambodia. It claimed the lives of 21 reporters.

The rebel communist Khmer Rouge broadcast warnings that foreign correspondents found in the capital Phnom Penh after its capture would be shot as "enemies of the people." That chilling prospect prompted the more cautious to leave immediately. Some like the CBC's Peter Kent stayed while rockets rained down on the capital and pulled out only hours before the city fell to the barbarous Khmer Rouge. Incredibly, a few

vvv

stayed to report on the capitulation, taking what was surely an unacceptable risk.

Among them were Jon Swain of the *London Times* and Syd Schanberg of the *New York Times*. Both men were captured by the rebels. With guns to their heads they were led away to what seemed like certain execution.

"At times like this," Jack Cahill wrote in *Words of War*, "a foreign correspondent must wonder why he isn't at home covering City Hall."

Shanberg and Swain survived to tell their shocking story of genocide of enormous, unbelievable proportions. The Khmer Rouge were systematically slaughtering their own people in an insane effort to establish a radical agrarian commune. Anywhere from one to two million people were exterminated. No one was sure how many, and what was worse, no one seemed to care all that much. The Americans were tired of Asia after the Vietnam war, and as some editors crassly put it, "gooks killing gooks isn't news." There were no TV pictures of this Asian holocaust. The attitude seemed to be that, if it's not on TV it's not happening.

Schanberg knew it was happening, risked his life to tell the world, and won the Pulitzer Prize for his coverage and insightful reporting. Yet, it was not until his story was told on the Hollywood screen in the movie *The Killing Fields* that the enormity of the crime made a real impact on the public consciousness.

Anyone who thought killing correspondents on purpose was only a Khmer Rouge aberration was wrong. The shooting-the-messenger syndrome resurfaced with a vengeance during the Yugoslav civil conflict in the early nineties, one of the dirtiest little wars any reporter was ever assigned to. Twenty journalists were killed during the first six months of that bitter ethnic feud. The Gulf War by contrast, with far more fire power and a much larger press contingent, counted nine correspondents among the dead.

Reporters who had covered wars from Vietnam to the Gulf had never seen anything like it. In the most brutal of conflicts combatants normally try to avoid shooting journalists. But in Yugoslavia they have been fair game, as snipers often single out correspondents as targets. The word PRESS on a car can draw fire, not prevent it.

Some correspondents, of course, tempted fate and lost. But even those who took normal precautions found that civil war is unlike any other war. There are no clear cut lines. The reporter accompanying federal troops became a target for the Croatian sniper in a nearby church steeple. Serbian snipers, convinced Western correspondents' reports tilted in favor of the Croats, didn't hesitate to open up on the first press car that drove into their scopes.

vv

Most correspondents quickly took down their press signs after Egon Scotland of Munich's *Süd deutsche Zeitung* was shot behind the wheel of his car as he drove into the Croatian town of Glina, held at the time by Serbian forces. His car was clearly marked as PRESS. Scotland bled to death before his colleague could get an ambulance.

Phil Davison, correspondent for Britain's *The Independent*, himself shot in the leg by a sniper, told a *Time* reporter, "In Yugoslavia, neither side gave a damn (about reporters)."

There are several schools of thought on how to handle dangerous assignments and the desirability of getting into the heat of action. Canadian reporter Oakland Ross feels that getting within earshot of combat is good enough, particularly for print reporters. His view is that a lot can be absorbed by staying behind the lines in the relative safety of the artillery units.

Another Canadian reporter agrees. Recalling his days as a WW II correspondent with the Canadian Army in Europe, he told me most of the combat reporters didn't think being in the centre of action helped to write about it. It was his contention that the infantryman's view of things is narrow and the chance of witnessing classic acts of heroism is low. He found it more productive to interview battle survivors later and get details like hometowns, names, etc. which he said are hard to come by in the heat of action.

Evelyn Waugh, novelist and a former foreign correspondent himself, aimed his devastating pen directly at reporters who shy away from action. In his satiric novel, *Scoop*, an editor is briefing the hero William Boot, prior to his first foreign posting, and tells him he'd be surprised how far war correspondents keep from the actual fighting. In fact, the novice reporter is told that the paper's most famous war correspondent never went near the fighting and gave them some of the most colorful "eyewitness stuff" they ever printed.

Waugh's fiction is not far removed from fact. In 1807 English lawyer Henry Crabb Robinson was commissioned by the *Times of London* to cover the Napoleonic Wars on the Continent. It is to be hoped that Robinson was a better lawyer than journalist. Apparently, he based his reports on what he read in the local paper without the benefit of personal observation or inquiry. His dispatch from Corunna in January 1809 after Napoleon's forces were pushed back neglected to inform his readers that the British commander-in-chief had been killed.

This is not to suggest that correspondents who choose to stay back from the action fabricate their reports. It does illustrate the differing attitudes of journalists covering dangerous assignments.

vv

Never going near the fighting wasn't the way people like CBC's Matthew Halton, NBC's Neil Davis or CBS's Walter Cronkite chose to cover combat.

Halton, according to his wartime colleague Charles Lynch, "wanted the sounds of battle and the only way to get them was to be there."

Davis too always insisted on getting to the extreme front line. Working from a distance with a telephoto lens wasn't getting the spontaneity of action he was after. It was Davis's nerves of steel that gave television around the world the pictures of a North Vietnamese tank crashing through the gates of the presidential palace in Saigon. His colleagues credit him with always weighing the story against the risk. On that particular occasion, he either judged correctly, or was extremely lucky. The thought went through his mind that the North Vietnamese would not fire on the lone cameraman recording this dramatic event for posterity. This time he was right.

Walter Cronkite was of a similar mould. In late September of 1944, Allied commanders attempted to end WW II in dramatic fashion—a large scale assault behind enemy lines in Holland. Part of the strategy was to drop an airborne army behind the lines using parachutes and gliders. On board, one of the more than 2 500 gliders used was a youthful *United Press* reporter named Walter Cronkite. He recalls how his glider came down so hard, helmets which everyone thought were hooked flew in all directions and seemed to present more danger than the shell fire. Cronkite first grabbed the closest helmet, then his bag with his typewriter and scrambled for the exit. He started crawling toward a canal which was the rendezvous point. Looking back, he saw half a dozen men following him. He had picked up the wrong helmet. The one he wore had two neat white lieutenant's stripes down the back.

Cronkite's penchant for seeing things first-hand didn't diminish with time. As a middle-aged anchorman at CBS he covered an aerial combat mission over Vietnam from inside a fighter-bomber.

Thirty years earlier, one of his predecessors at CBS had done much the same thing in Europe. Edward R. Murrow once went on an RAF bombing mission over Berlin, in which only half the planes returned.

There are of course hot spots where it is risky for Western journalists to venture and where news agencies depend on local staff for coverage. Lebanon is still such a place. Here foreign correspondents, particularly males, have been prime targets for hostage-taking by radical Muslim factions. High profile journalists like Terry Anderson of *Associated Press*, held for nearly seven years, are the currency used by Muslim extremists to bargain for the release of Arab prisoners held in Israel.

vvv

In other cases, journalists are captured to protest against the foreign policies of their governments. British television journalist John McCarthy, released after being held hostage for five years, was captured in retaliation for Prime Minister Margaret Thatcher allowing U.S. bombers to use British bases in raids on Libya. McCarthy was 29 when he was abducted in Beirut. He was on his very first foreign assignment.

The dangers of being taken hostage have lessened, but as every veteran Middle East correspondent knows, the only thing that's predictable about that part of the world, is that it is totally unpredictable. If it's not hostage-taking it will be something else.

In the final analysis the decision to risk or not to risk lies with the correspondent and to a lesser extent his or her editor. But one fact remains, for the good journalist getting information second-hand is second-best. A reporter can interview people later who tell you, "Yes, I was there, this is what I saw, this is what was said." Sometimes they are right, sometimes wrong, sometimes half-right.

For journalists, the most euphoric feeling is being able to say, "This is what happened. I was there. I saw it. It was worth the risk!" Nothing beats being there.

vvvvvvvvvvvvvvvvvvvvvvvvvvvvvvvvvvvvvvvvvvvvvvvvvvvvvvvvvvvvv

The Inter American Press Association, alarmed at the increasing dangers to journalists in the Americas, asked reporters and editors to suggest ways journalists could protect themselves or reduce the danger inherent in covering perilous assignments. A pamphlet, "Surviving Dangerous Assignments," has been widely circulated since its publication in 1985. The following is an edited version of the pamphlet.

Surviving Dangerous Assignments

Suggestions will be valid in particular situations. Above all, correspondents must use their good judgment and common sense under varying conditions. But in general, these "Do's and Don'ts," judiciously applied, can cut the risks of doing your job in hostile terrain.

1. You are more important than the story. No story is worth your life.

2. If you are clearly threatened, get out as fast as you can.

3. If authorities can't guarantee your safety, leave the country.

4. Never carry a gun or other weapon.

5. Never point your finger; it can be mistaken for a gun.

6. Know the country, the region and the people involved.

vvv

7. Know the language at least well enough to identify yourself and to talk to local residents.

8. Always carry complete identification papers.

9. If you are in an unfamiliar area, travel with other journalists who know it well.

10. Know all your journalistic colleagues in dangerous situations. Strangers may not be what they seem.

11. Outcries against abuse provide protection. Resist abuse by authorities and always protest such abuse of yourself and other professionals. But don't become abusive yourself.

12. Avoid unknown risks. Vague promises of a story often come from persons who can't guarantee your safety.

13. Stories in remote locations far from authority and medical assistance present added risk.

14. Do not masquerade as other than what you are. It raises suspicions and creates risk for other professionals.

15. Under no circumstances accept compensation from or do work for a non-journalistic or government information-gathering or government intelligence agency.

16. A professional must maintain a standard of truth despite risks and dangers. Some stories are worth more risk than others.

17. Avoid bias for one side or another. Do not cross the line between journalist and active participant.

18. Weigh what you know about the risks against the possible benefits of a story. Often, a story is just as good if covered from a distance.

19. Distinguish between risk and present danger. Avoid obvious danger and don't take undue risks. Often discussing this with friends and colleagues can help.

20. Avoid reporting from both sides of a conflict if possible. Crossing from one side to the other often is dangerous.

21. Always carry a white flag.

22. Always use extreme care in selecting competent locals as drivers, guides, etc. Their presence of mind is a protection.

23. Mark your car clearly as "press" in the local language.

24. Use two cars where practical in case one breaks down.

vv

25. Never wash your car. Unwanted tampering can be detected easier on a dirty car.

26. Talk to local residents as much as possible and listen to their advice.

27. Dress appropriately. This will vary. Sometimes you will want to blend into a crowd; at other times, you may want obviously not to be one of the group.

28. Never wear olive green or anything that makes you look like a soldier.

29. Let your desk or editors know where you are at all times, where you are going and when you expect to return.

30. Let your colleagues at the hotel know the same thing.

31 When confronted by hostile persons, identify yourself in their language and attempt to convey ideas about what you are doing.

32. If guerillas at roadblocks ask you for a "war tax," give something. It shouldn't be much, but it can avoid unpleasantness.

33. Never run checkpoints; never display maps openly.

34. Carry a short-wave radio to keep track of developments on the BBC or other reliable stations.

35. Fill your bathtub with water in case water system cut off.

36. Think through your mission, how best to get the story. For example, do you risk sniper fire or should you be more circumspect?

37. Keep an active mind regarding risks and ask yourself questions.

38. All you have in dangerous situations are your wits and knowledge of the area. Your editor and the Geneva Convention normally can't help you.

39. Make certain you know the local meaning of symbols like white flags, red flags, whistles, gestures, etc.

40. Evaluate your physical characteristics. Don't attempt something you lack stamina to complete.

41. Make certain your employer carries insurance that will adequately provide if you are injured or killed.

42. Editors should always be aware of the risks reporters or photographers are running. They also bear responsibility and should not push unreasonably.

Anything You Can Do . . .

> They may think she's a whore, but often they will talk to her more
> openly than to a male reporter.
>
> — Linda Ellerbee

MORE WOMEN THAN MEN ARE NOW ENTERING JOURNAL-
ism in Canada and the United States, both as beginning reporters and
journalism students. The field of international reporting is, however, still
very much a man's domain. That's changing rapidly in North America
(considerably slower elsewhere)—we have regularly seen the by-lines of
Edith Terry, *Globe & Mail*, Tokyo; Aileen McCabe, *Southam News*,
Amman; Caryle Murphy, *Washington Post*, Cairo; and hear broadcast
sign offs like Jeannette Matthey, *CBC News*, Moscow and Sheila
MacVicar, *ABC* News, Baghdad.

It's been a long time coming. UPI reporter Joyce Fairbairn (now a
Canadian Senator) broke the male barrier in the Parliamentary Press
Gallery in Ottawa in 1962, but only after considerable opposition from
the gallery's dinosaurs.* The first time I saw Joyce in the press room she
was berating a young male reporter who had just put his foot in it by
volunteering the opinion that the Parliamentary Press Gallery badly
needed someone who could do "women's" pieces from the Hill.

Over the next 10 years Fairbairn would prove that she was no cookie
correspondent. She was continually on the cutting edge of major stories,
from the rise and fall of John Diefenbaker and the turbulent Pearson years
to the flowering of Pierre Trudeau.

Fairbairn made journalistic history. It would be another 10 years (1971)
before the National Press Club in Washington would lift its 40-year ban
on women members.** The distinction of being the first female member
of the NPC went to a woman with the peculiarly American moniker of
Esther Van Wagoner Tufty. When she signed her membership card she
was just turning 75. Tufty had accumulated an impressive journalistic

---

* Canadian broadcast journalists had an equally difficult time gaining gallery
  membership. Sam Ross, representing a group of private broadcasters, was
  admitted only a few years before Fairbairn.

**Women had, however, covered the White House. The first full-time female
  correspondent to cover presidential activities was appointed in 1966.

vvv

record. She flew the Berlin airlift on top of a cargo of coal, was a WW II correspondent before that and subsequently reported on the Korean and Vietnam wars.

Impressive as these first are, the real pioneering work by women in journalism occurred in the late 1800s and early 1900s.

At the beginning of the twentieth century there were fewer than 40 women journalists in all of Canada compared with some 800 men. They wrote about cooking, sewing, raising children and anything else that fell into the homemaking category. They were not expected (nor allowed) to write about anything else. Politics, economics, foreign affairs, wars, were all off limits.

As is invariably the case, there were rebels, women in both Canada and the United States who defied the status of second-class journalistic citizenship and broke into other reporting areas, including the foreign field. In Canada, Kathleen Blake Coleman, columnist and editor of the women's page in the *Toronto Mail Empire* was one of these. Kit Coleman, as she signed her by-lines, chafed under the restraints of doing "women's" items. Much to the dismay of her editors she set out to prove that women too were interested in politics, trade, the stock market, Darwin's theory of evolution, and generally the world around them. Kit certainly was. She became the first woman to be accredited as a war correspondent. Her paper sent her to Cuba where Teddy Roosevelt's Roughriders were doing battle in the Spanish-American War. Her editors of course didn't expect her to do any serious reporting, only feature stuff or "guff" as it was called in those days. The real news was to be left to the men.

In spite of her accreditation in Washington, getting to Cuba was no easy matter. The U.S. State Department and her male colleagues conspired to keep her holed up in Tampa, waiting for sea transport to Cuba. The war was all but over when she finally arrived there, but she managed to file some insightful aftermath pieces. Kit was to discover, as thousands of reporters have since, that dangers inherent in foreign reporting aren't always apparent. She contracted malaria while in Cuba, and never fully recovered her health. She died at age 59 in 1915.

At about the time of Kit's death, a plucky self-made Texan journalist was preparing to be the first female correspondent to cover WW I. Peggy Hall of the *El Paso Times* thrived on adventure. During the Mexican border fighting, her paper let her do offbeat articles on the war. Always near the action, she caught the eye of the American commander General John Pershing. Pershing was impressed with the gutsy young reporter who marched with his troops, roughed it in the field, and still managed to maintain her femininity.

vv

When Pershing took the American Expeditionary Force to France in WW I, who should appear at his headquarters one day but the indomitable Peggy Hall. The austere general welcomed his unexpected guest as "a breath from home" and gave her what he had denied all the male correspondents, a personal interview.

Neither her connections in high places, her popularity with the troops, nor the fact that the other papers were picking up the "Peggy" by-lines could save her career. The all-male correspondents corps mounted a relentless campaign against her, claiming she was using her feminine wiles to get her exclusive interviews. She failed to get accreditation and was forced to return home.

Nevertheless, Kit and Peggy had blazed the path for the next generation of women correspondents—mostly Americans. Aigrid Schultz became the first female to run a foreign news bureau. In 1926 she was appointed chief Central European correspondent for the *Chicago Tribune*, a job she held until 1941.

Schultz became an authority on German affairs and was among the first to expose the rising Nazi menace through incriminating interviews with leading Nazis, including Hitler and Goering. Her insightful articles impressed the executives at the *Mutual Broadcasting System* and they did the unthinkable for the time: they put Schultz on the air with a weekly news commentary. It was her voice on Mutual that announced the outbreak of war in Europe.

Of her prewar front-page stories and radio commentaries she expressed the hope that they had encouraged editors to "entrust important posts to the female of the species."

Dorothy Thompson was one of Schultz's contemporaries who also ended up as head of a news bureau. Her devastating reports and analysis of the Nazis gave her the distinction of being the first woman foreign correspondent to be expelled from Europe when the Nazis assumed power. She also ran into trouble at home. Her paper, the *New York Post*, dropped her column when in 1947 she came out against the creation of the Israeli state.

Helen Kirkpatrick was another accomplished reporter who broke into international work at the outbreak of WW II. In 1939, she became the first woman foreign correspondent for the *Chicago Daily News*. It was a daring decision. "But," she recalls, "they wanted me, so they had to change their policy because I wasn't about to change my sex." Once established in Europe, Kirkpatrick became a regular contributor to such influential papers as the *London Daily Telegraph, Manchester Guardian*, and the *New York Herald Tribune*. The suggestion by some male reporters

vv

that women use sexuality to get stories was prevalent in Kirkpatrick's time and persists to this day. It's an unfair accusation.

Gwen Dew of the *Detroit News* didn't play up her sex on the eve of the fall of Hong Kong in 1941. She calmly arranged a one-woman news conference with a three-man Japanese military delegation which was demanding the unconditional surrender of British, Indian and Canadian forces holding the British colony. She confronted the arrogant and menacing trio with the kind of blunt questioning the officers were quite unaccustomed to. Dew stayed on to cover the subsequent battle which saw some of the worst atrocities committed by the Japanese during WW II. She was captured and imprisoned for the duration of the war.

As more women, mostly American and British, moved into traditional male jobs it was inevitable that many of them would, like Gwen Dew, find themselves covering combat. One of the more illustrious was Marguerite Higgins of the *New York Herald Tribune*. Higgins was attractive, intelligent and above all ambitious. She launched her international career during WW II. She was the first reporter at the Nazi death camp at Dachau after it was liberated by American troops. Five years later she plunged with great relish into coverage of the Korean War. Her colleagues say she took a lot of chances, being the first to report on the initial fiasco at Pusan where green American troops fresh from occupation duty in Japan were cut to pieces by a steam roller North Korean advance. She wrote, "I saw young Americans turn and bolt in battle, or throw down their arms cursing their government for what they thought was embroilment in a hopeless cause." She won a Pulitzer Prize for her work in Korea.

Higgins seemed intoxicated on danger. She often said she had no plans to marry until she found a man "who is as exciting as war." Apparently she found one. She married General William Hall, USAF. Married life, however, didn't quench her penchant for war reporting. She was drawn as if by a magnet to Vietnam.

But times had changed. Higgins' style of reporting didn't fit in with the new critical journalistic thinking. Higgins accused those who asked unpleasant questions of trying to sabotage the war effort. Time had passed her by and Vietnam was to be her last assignment. It also claimed her life. Like Canadian Kit Coleman 75 years earlier, she contracted a tropical disease in Vietnam and died on her return to the United States. She was 45.

The list of women war correspondents is, if not long, illustrious. Some of the more notable, in addition to those already mentioned, include: Georgie Anne Geyer, Dickie Chapelle (killed in Vietnam), Alice Leone Moats, Jurate Kazikas and Aline Mosby, all Americans; Kate Webb, an

vv

Australian; and Britishers Marina Warner, Charlotte Haldane and Virginia Cowles.

No list of outstanding women in international reporting would be complete without the name Margaret Bourke-White, the news photographer who made Stalin smile. Bourke-White was the first female photojournalist for *Life* magazine. In 1941, while covering the battle for Moscow in WW II, she was granted a photo interview with the stern Soviet dictator. The German Army was only a few miles from the Kremlin, so Stalin could be forgiven for not being in a jovial frame of mind. Nevertheless, Bourke-White's ridiculous antics to get the right camera angle induced a broad smile from the mustached face that struck cold terror into the heart of every Soviet citizen from peasant to marshall of the Army.

Kit Coleman's sterling example notwithstanding, Canadian women failed to make a significant impact on international reporting, particularly war corresponding until quite recently. The CBC's Anna Maria Tremonte, Sheila MacVicar, now with ABC, and Aileen McCabe of *Southam News* are but a few of the Canadian women making their mark in foreign reporting.

Attitudes are changing, but editors still hesitate to send women into combat zones. Some women don't wait. Caryle Murphy of the *Washington Post* decided things were too quiet in her Cairo bureau so she caught a plane to Kuwait when Saddam Hussein started making threatening noises to invade. The timely move made Murphy the only Western reporter to have what she described as a "front row seat for witnessing a small nation being crushed by its larger neighbor." Murphy managed to evade Iraqi troops for a month, filing regular dispatches through facilities provided by friendly embassies. Eventually she joined a convoy making a daring escape across the Iraqi-patrolled desert to the Saudi Arabian border.*

When the Gulf War broke out, women correspondents provided the public in both Europe and North America with some of the most lucid and insightful reportage of the war. Charlayne Hunter Gault reported for PBS in Dhahran, Saudi Arabia, Aileen McCabe of *Southam News* in Amman and Betsy Aaron of CBS from "behind enemy lines" in Baghdad. After leaving Baghdad, Antonia Rados of *Austrian Television* was able to give the world one of the first comprehensive uncensored pictures of life in Baghdad under air bombardment. Linda Pattillo of ABC drove

---

* Murphy won a Pulitzer Prize for her reports out of occupied Kuwait.

vv

across the Saudi-Kuwaiti border with the Second Marine Division on day one of the liberation of Kuwait, to become the only woman journalist to report from the front lines. CBS's Martha Teichner slugged it out in the barren desert for weeks bivouacked with a dug in mechanized infantry unit. "If she wanted privacy," said colleague Arthur Kent of NBC, "she had to put up a blanket out in the sand." The Pattillos & Teichners were a decided minority, so there were the inevitable complaints that too few women had been given combat assignments. "Where were the women reporters to put a female perspective on the war?" asked a female reporter during a panel discussion of war coverage at the 1991 Banff Television Festival. "How does a female perspective of a war differ from a man's perspective?" asked panelist Brigit Weidinger, media page editor of Germany's *Süddentsche Zeitung.* "An argument perhaps can be made that more women should have been assigned," she went on, "but I can't see a woman viewing the war any differently than a man." Rados, and all the other reporters who worked out of the Iraqi capital during the war, showed a great deal of courage. The danger came not so much from the bombing itself, as from angry crowds gathered around the sites where bombs had killed civilians. On several occasions police had to keep Iraqi citizens from attacking television camera crews. It should be noted, however, that under the circumstances the Iraqis showed immense restraint. Instances of outright hostility and animosity toward the media reporting for countries raining bombs on the Iraqis' heads were rare.

Assigning women to combat zones still presents problems—especially in the Middle East where attitudes toward women are primitive. Women correspondents accept that some situations may demand the jettisoning of modesty. Devout Muslims invariably do not. Dress requirements vary from country to country. Normal western dress is acceptable in Iraq, Jordan, Lebanon, Egypt and Syria. In Saudi Arabia, Iran and Yemen, traditional Muslim dress for women is often enforced by roving religious police squads.

Reporters didn't present a problem for the Saudis before the war. Except for special occasions correspondents were not allowed into the country. Women never. The Gulf War changed all that. Reporters, including women, were admitted, but were expected to behave the way Saudi women did. French language CBC reporter Genevieve Rossier found out the hard way. A deathly hush fell over a Riyadh restaurant when she and a male companion entered. "Out, out," the distraught manager shouted. Rossier was also unceremoniously ejected from a "men's" park in the centre of the dusty capital. Rossier's adventures weren't over yet. When a gust of wind blew open her full length black *obaya* to reveal

vv

colored trousers and blouse, the religious police descended on her with abuse, whips at the ready until she was properly covered up.

The Saudis rationalized the presence of women correspondents as they did the idea of the female American soldiers who came to their defense. They were simply designated as males with female features.

Women correspondents working in the Middle East do however get some breaks. "In Lebanon," says Janice Turner of *South Magazine*, "women journalists had the edge over their male counterparts." Tradition decrees that women are inferior to men and must be patronized and treated with deference. Turner says she was often treated as though she didn't exist. At checkpoints, she could feel the tension drain from masked gunmen when they saw it was a woman walking toward them. She never carried the walletfull of official passes from the different factions like her male counterparts did. A standard international press card and a passport got her wherever she wanted to go.

Women correspondents got a break of sorts from the Pentagon during the Gulf War too. Recognizing that out-of-shape reporters could jeopardize their own safety as well as those of soldiers escorting them to combat zones, the military ordered physical fitness tests. Male journalists under 40 were required to run 2.4 kilometres in 15 minutes and 30 seconds, do 33 push-ups in two minutes and 32 sit-ups in two minutes. Women in the same age group were given an extra one minute and 45 seconds to make the run. Push-ups were reduced to 13 and sit-ups to 30. (Obviously those who set up the tests didn't take into account that bullets have no gender.)

Women get other breaks in the news business. Francine Bastien, who has worked for Radio-Canada out of London and Washington, found that male newsmakers gave interviews more readily to women than to men because they assumed women wouldn't ask the tough questions. Aileen McCabe, now general manager of Southam News, discovered that Arab youths in Gaza would throw rocks at male reporters, but leave the women alone. Working out of China for the Globe & Mail, Jan Wong says female reporters generally have greater access to other women than men do. Certainly, she says, a woman will confide things to another woman she would never tell a man.

But being a woman in the field has drawbacks too. At this writing, a female reporter for Southam News in Bosnia has hired bodyguards to protect her from harassment and possible rape by soldiers at roadblocks.

Discrimination against women is not confined to the Middle East. It crops up in the most unexpected places. In supposedly enlightened Japan where the ascent to economic superpower status has further nourished that country's chronic male arrogance, women reporters are still finding it difficult to work on an equal footing with men. Newspaper reporter Aki

vv

Omori found that out when she was barred from covering the opening ceremonies of a newly built tunnel. Construction companies wouldn't allow her near the site, insisting that her presence would offend the mountain goddess—not to mention some chauvinist Japanese males.

International news reporting for women still isn't easy. Sooner or later the female correspondent has to make a difficult choice. Stay in one place so she can meet and get to know a mate and perhaps have children, or remain on the road with only a slim chance of forming a serious relationship. Those who stick with international reporting tend only to meet and socialize with other correspondents. When two correspondents do marry there's no guarantee that their respective employers will locate them at the same base.

Male correspondents take for granted that wives will tend to hearth and home wherever that happens to be, enrol the kids in school, pay the bills and do whatever else needs doing while he travels the globe. How many men would stand for a reversal of that role if their wives were foreign correspondents? If they were assigned to a war zone? That problem probably explains why the vast majority of women in the news business work in local or national newsrooms. Surprisingly though, there's no shortage of women lining up for international reporting jobs, many with sterling qualifications.

One top-notch national reporter who found "those trench coats mighty appealing" was NBC's Linda Ellerbee. She got in line for an international job then quickly got out of line when she gave the situation a little more thought. "I had two small children at the time," she wrote in her book *And So It Goes*, "and it seemed less than motherly of me to plunk down the kids in a country where they might not speak the language while I hotfooted it to the nearest airport." Ellerbee understood all too well that correspondents who go abroad with a family must face the prospect of raising children who can develop roots in their home country and the danger that they will never form an attachment to any country of distinct cultural identity. Odds are that women who choose a foreign career won't stay in the international game. Nor should they. The burnout rate for both women and men is high because of professional pressures, bad food, little sleep, physical danger and the emotional exhaustion of almost daily confrontation with human misery.

All these negatives notwithstanding, the trend set by the Colemans and Halls at the turn of the century will continue. As the number of women entering journalism grows, so will their numbers in the field of international reporting.

Cloaks, Daggers and Trench Coats

"I was wondering if Algy would send me [to Ishmaelia] as a spy?"

"Not a chance."

"No?"

"Foregonners. Algy's been sacking ten spies a day for weeks. It's a grossly overcrowded profession. Why don't you go as a war correspondent?"

—Scoop, by Evelyn Waugh.

IN MANY COUNTRIES ESPIONAGE AND JOURNALISM ARE indeed interchangeable professions. The Russians, recognized masters in the spy business, have had a reputation for being the most blatant abusers of journalism as a cover for their intelligence agents.* The British probably come a close second, although the French and Americans among others, have also paraded intelligence operatives as newsmen.

"Drafting" journalists and others in the communications industry into intelligence service became a well-established practice just before WWII, particularly in Britain. Fredrick Voight of the *Manchester Guardian* doubled as a spy and Vienna correspondent for his paper.

Alexander Korda, the British movie mogul, put his film company at the disposal of intelligence as a cover. Malcolm Muggeridge, esteemed reporter and commentator with the *Guardian*, signed on for espionage duties.

Journalists working as war correspondents were also expected to do their duty for intelligence. Charles Lynch in *You Can't Print That* tells how he and other reporters designated for the D-Day landings in 1944 were rounded up without warning by military intelligence in England and hustled aboard a train headed for Scotland. It was all part of an elaborate exercise to fool the German spies into thinking the invasion of the European mainland was on. The reporters were used as decoys because, Lynch says, "war correspondents were the most visible component of the Allied force, some of them more famous than the generals." Aboard that train were Ernie Pyle, Alan Moorehead and Wes Gallager (all famous American journalists at the time).

---

* The Russian Federation Security Ministry, formerly the KGB, has pledged not to use foreign correspondents as spies.

vv

The most notorious of the British journalist-spies was Kim Philby the long-time Soviet mole in MI6. Philby got his baptism of fire literally as a Soviet agent in the late thirties in Spain. He was an accredited correspondent for *The Times* in London, attached to General Franco's forces. What better position from which to report Franco's military operations to the Soviets, who were backing the opposing Republican side.

Philby's performance pleased all concerned. *The Times* was apparently satisfied with his graphic reports from the front lines, the Soviets (and consequently the Spanish Republican Army) were fully apprised of Franco's moves, and Franco personally decorated the brave British journalist after he had been wounded, paradoxically by an artillery shell supplied by his Soviet employers. It was the beginning of an incredible juggling act that Philby was to perform for nearly three more decades.

At the outbreak of WW II, *The Times* sent its star reporter across the Channel as their correspondent accredited to the British Army Headquarters in France. This, at a time when Philby was still on the Soviet intelligence payroll.

Philby's reporting job in France didn't last long. With the help of his old friend Guy Burgess, also a Soviet agent and sometime BBC Talks department commentator, Philby was able to leave journalism for a more promising career in MI6, Britain's foreign intelligence service. Philby was now a full-fledged double agent, a role he carried out with devastating effect throughout the crucial early years of the Cold War.

Suspicion that Philby was a Soviet mole triggered a government investigation. But no hard evidence was found to nail him down. Philby was officially cleared and put back on the MI6 payroll, this time as a lowly field officer, but again with the cover of a journalist. *The Observer* apparently had no compunction about making this compromised British intelligence agent its man in Beirut. And it was his work as a journalist in the Middle East that finally did him in.

In 1962, Flora Solomon, a prewar friend of Philby's, read some of his reports in the papers. She was decidedly unhappy with the slant of his articles, which she considered anti-Israel. She decided to blow the whistle on her old friend. Solomon passed the word to MI5, Britain's domestic intelligence service, that Philby had once tried to recruit her as a Soviet agent. With that revelation all earlier suspicions were confirmed. Philby's career as a spy-journalist was over.

But again, he slipped through the net, probably with a little help from his friends at MI6. He disappeared from Beirut, apparently aboard a Soviet freighter and surfaced six months later in Moscow.

For the next 25 years Philby was all but invisible. Like a rare bird he was occasionally sighted by Western correspondents. On one occasion

vv

an American broadcast journalist standing at a urinal in the men's room at Moscow's National Hotel bar glanced up to see none other than the ruddy-faced Philby standing next to him. Philby was in full flow and the reporter was in a perfect position to conduct an impromptu interview. The master double agent wouldn't have divulged anything of consequence anyway, but the reporter was so rattled by the impossible situation he only managed to blurt out a few mundane pleasantries.

Another Philby sighting occurred several months later when David Levy, a Canadian newspaper reporter, spotted the unmistakable Philby profile in the liquor line up at one of Moscow's foreign currency shops. The only information Levy was able to glean was that Philby's favorite scotch was Johnny Walker Black Label and that he was accompanied by a KGB guard who doubled as a chauffeur.

In May of 1988 Kim Philby died in his sleep and was given a full military burial by the KGB to whom he had been loyally devoted his entire adult life.

The old Soviet Union expected every citizen to do his or her duty when it came to national security—or what the state perceived to be its national security. Its journalists, foreign-based or domestic, were no exception. The list of Soviet journalists expelled from other countries "for activities unrelated to journalism" is too long to list here. Some expulsions are more memorable than others.

In Ottawa, three Soviet correspondents were expelled during a 10 year period from the mid-sixties to the mid-seventies for espionage. Of these the most interesting character was an amiable reporter for *Pravda* named Konstantin Geyvandov. Geyvandov's primary role was not to keep Pravda's Soviet readership informed about Canadian affairs, but to gather information for his real bosses, the KGB. A burly bear-like man, Geyvandov was quite unlike his dour Soviet colleagues. The *Toronto Sun's* usually perceptive columnist Douglas Fisher described him as "big, silly, amiable and dumb," a genial chap who was most unlikely to be a spy. Geyvandov, of course, was anything but dumb. Like other Soviet journalists based in Canada, Geyvandov succeeded in getting Canadian journalists to do seemingly innocent jobs for him. (Free-lancers were especially vulnerable.)

The usual ploy was to ask a willing reporter to prepare profiles on members of Parliament and key civil servants. The tasks seemed innocent enough, although warning flags should have gone up immediately in the minds of reporters he approached, because the information the Soviets were willing to pay for is readily available in the Canadian Parliamentary Guide and any number of other government publications. Soviet journalists have the same access to this material as anyone else.

vvv

The profiles of course were merely the hook. Once a reporter accepted money, he or she found it more difficult to turn down the next assignment, which could be digging up dirt on a member of the cabinet or senior public servants to be used as potential blackmail.

In the case of Geyvandov, a confidential RCMP document at the time described the Soviet journalist's operations in this way.

> Active in the development of channels of influence are Soviet press representatives who frequent the House of Commons and National Press Gallery. A Pravda representative, Konstantin Yervandovich Geyvandov, managed to persuade a Canadian journalist to act on behalf of Soviet interests when reporting Canadian political events. In addition, Geyvandov, in a surreptitious, clandestine and intelligence-oriented way, regularly obtained from the journalist an assessment of certain events which were likely to have an impact on future Canadian policy. As a result of these activities, Geyvandov was denied a visa in 1974 to re-enter Canada following a holiday in the USSR.

Normally, in such a situation, the Soviets would retaliate by kicking a Canadian correspondent out of Moscow. But, at the time of Geyvandov's expulsion there was only one Canadian reporter based in the USSR. The Russians have anywhere from four to six journalists in Canada at any given time, so they passed on the usual diplomatic game of tit for tat. There simply were not enough Canadian players on the board to play the game.

The RCMP too, when it was responsible for internal security, did not hesitate to try co-opting journalists to assist their surveillance operations. Several years after the Geyvandov affair, the RCMP tried to recruit an attractive female journalist to befriend and report on an Ottawa-based Russian. Kitty McKinsey, of the *Ottawa Citizen*, patiently listened to the RCMP officer's proposal over lunch, then much to the force's embarrassment, promptly returned to her paper and wrote the whole story.

Soviet agents were sometimes equally clumsy in their efforts to compromise foreign correspondents in the USSR. The following is an excerpt from my diary notes while working as the CBC's man in Moscow.

> *May 11/70*
>
> Got a phone call today from a woman who described herself as a University of Moscow Ph.D. candidate. Says she's working on a thesis about nations sharing the Arctic or some such thing. Goes on to say she understands I covered Canadian North before coming to USSR. Could I give her an interview about development in our North. Agree to do so. Mention same to Margaret (my Soviet secretary/translator). She sniffs that caller no university student. Didn't elaborate or explain.

vvv

May 14/70

"University student" arrived in office today. More mature than I expected. Mid-thirties? Name is Galena. Knowledge of North, theirs and ours, seems sketchy. After a few elementary questions asks about American forces in Canadian Arctic. Jokingly tell her I'll brief her on our Arctic defenses (practically non-existent except for DEW line) in exchange for info on Soviet Arctic installations. Interview ends. Obviously little progress made on "thesis" today.

November 14/70

Attended Canadian Embassy reception last night. Number of Soviet foreign ministry people there, all from U.S.- Canada desk. As usual no info. of news value. Surprise, Surprise! Galena there with husband Vladimir (didn't catch last name) foreign ministry official on Canadian desk. Finally managed to corner her, find out how "thesis" coming along. Flatly denied that she ever laid eyes on me or that she was studying at Moscow U. Very cool. Excused herself and headed in general direction of washroom. Recall interview with RCMP counter intelligence in Ottawa before leaving about femme fatale provocateurs, etc. Disappointed. Expected someone more mysterious and glamorous.

During the Brezhnev years, entrapment of foreign correspondents was common practice. Personal dossiers were kept by the KGB on all reporters to be used as blackmail if, in the opinion of authorities, their reports were "unfriendly" to the Soviet Union. Much of the information for their dossiers came from the reporter's own Soviet staff who briefed the KGB regularly on their employer's activities.

The case of an American correspondent for a major news magazine was fairly typical. After several warnings from the foreign ministry press section, he continued writing reports on the Soviet dissidents, chronic food shortages and other less attractive aspects of Soviet life. Not content to simply expel him, the Soviets released on the English Tass wire all personal information they'd gathered on him. Allegations such as black market currency dealings and sexual indiscretions figured prominently in the exposé.

The KGB operated on the theory that if enough mud is thrown, some of it is bound to stick. In spite of the KGB's reputation for disseminating inaccurate information, public revelations of a reporter's peccadillos, real or imagined, often resulted in marital break up and in some cases career demotions.

In at least one instance involving an American correspondent, the Russians appeared to have a strong case of a reporter dabbling in espionage. The CIA insisted that reporter Nicholas Daniloff was not a

vv

spy and had been falsely arrested. The KGB was just as adamant that he was a spy and furthermore said they'd caught him red-handed in a sting operation. When Daniloff was released by Moscow in 1986 Soviet spy Gennadi Zakharov was released simultaneously by Washington. President Reagan still insisted there had been no spy swap. The Soviets played along with the American's game by insisting that their man wasn't a spy either.

The Soviet media were the first beneficiaries of glasnost. Domestic reporters found themselves able to criticize politicians, bureaucrats and the Communist Party itself with near impunity. The new openness also spread to foreign reporters, giving them unprecedented access free of suspicions of espionage. Welcome as these developments are, there is no guarantee that they are permanent, or that there will be similar breakthroughs soon in hard line totalitarian states like China, North Korea, Vietnam and Cuba.

During the Vietnam war, a number of South Vietnamese journalists worked two jobs: one as a reporter in the pay of the American press, the other as an informant for Hanoi.

In 1981, Arnaud de Borchgrave gave testimony to that effect before the U.S. Senate sub committee on security and terrorism. Specifically, the former senior editor of *Newsweek* told the committee that a Vietnamese reporter for *Time*, Pham Xuan An, had been an agent for Hanoi. No evidence was produced, though, that he passed on misinformation through his magazine. An freely admits to having been an agent, but vehemently denies that he ever planted a story. He feared it would be too apparent and jeopardize his job both as a reporter and an intelligence agent.

In a totally frank interview with CBS correspondent Morley Safer, An said the information he gathered for the Viet Cong was exactly what *Time* expected, but in more detail—strengths of ARVN (South Vietnamese) units, commander capabilities, political information, who could be bribed and who couldn't, etc. Every few months he would secretly brief the Viet Cong.

The Soviet system of control and surveillance of foreign correspondents was eventually adopted by the communist government in China. But while Moscow has dropped most of its foreign media restrictions and at least partially dismantled its all-pervasive surveillance apparatus, the Chinese system is not only still in place, it has been tightened considerably since the Tiananmen Square massacre in the spring of 1989.

New regulations issued in early 1990 after martial law was lifted, ban foreign journalists from any actions the government deems harmful to Chinese society or what it considers to be intelligence gathering. The

vv

most sweeping of the new rules says, foreign correspondents and news agencies must observe journalistic ethics, and must not distort facts, fabricate rumors or use improper means in their reporting.

> *Foreign correspondents and news agencies must not engage in activities that are incompatible with their status, or those that endanger state security, national unification or the public interest of Chinese society.*

The rules specified that the new regulations would be interpreted by the Chinese authorities. The country has always regulated foreign reporters and the new rules were mostly a restatement of what was already on the books. The restatement made it clear however, that the restrictions would be more rigorously enforced and more narrowly interpreted.

The People's Republic of China has expanded its use of journalists as intelligence agents and vice versa. In Hong Kong, the official Chinese news agency, *Xinhua*, is now ensconced in its own office tower. The size of its staff is out of all proportion to the number of reporters required to cover the British crown colony. Few in Hong Kong, least of all the departing British, are under any illusions as to what the news agency is really up to—gathering intelligence dossiers for the day in 1997 when the colony reverts to Chinese rule.

The way in which intelligence agencies use journalists for their own purposes is often callous and at times nothing short of tragic.

In May of 1984, a group of foreign journalists was making its way by boat up a jungle river along the Nicaraguan-Costa Rican border. Their destination was La Penca, the remote redoubt of renegade Contra leader Eden Pastora. He was hot news at the time, and an invitation to cover one of his rare news conferences was not to be missed by anyone covering the Sandanista-Contra jungle war.

Pastora's two-storey wooden house, concealed by heavy tropical foliage along the river bank, was not easily accessible. And with good reason. He had enemies other than the Sandanistas in Managua whom he had been battling for years. His hatred of Daniel Ortega's Sandanista regime should have made him a friend of the American CIA and the staunchly anticommunist Reagan administration in Washington; it would have if he hadn't been such a maverick. Pastora refused to operate under the umbrella of the CIA supported and sanctioned Contra movement in Nicaragua. He preferred to run his own show, and thus in the eyes of the CIA and its client Contra leadership, Pastora was a direct threat to the success of the Reagan administration's determined efforts to topple Ortega's regime.

Included in the group of reporters, TV cameramen and news photographers on the motor launch was a newcomer to the press party. He

vvv

described himself as a freelance news photographer, and quickly be-friended his seat-mate, a Swedish TV cameraman named Peter Tor-gensen. No one, including Pastora's men, inquired about his credentials or which organization he was connected with. (He carried a Danish passport, later found to be fake.) Nor did anyone pay any particular attention to the swarthy young man as the news conference got under way and he pushed his heavy metal camera close to Pastora's table.

Seconds later the "freelance photographer" casually walked out of the house. Using a remote detonating device he triggered an explosion that nearly demolished the building. Pastora walked away from the blast unhurt, but three journalists died. Seventeen were injured, some crippled for life.

One of those seriously hurt was Susan Morgan, a British-born reporter for *Newsweek.* During her many months of therapy and recuperation, the incident became an obsession with her. Why, she asked herself, did it happen? Who was responsible? The Sandanistas? Pastora's contra oppo-nents? Miami Cuban ultra-rightists? The CIA? Whoever it was obviously deemed journalists to be expendable to the cause, whatever the cause was. She, as an innocent human being, was seen as someone of no conse-quence.

Morgan was angry, and more than that she was determined to track down the person or persons responsible. Who wanted Pastora dead, and was willing to take as many journalists as necessary with him?

Morgan went back to Central America with a British TV documentary crew in an attempt to pick up the terrorist's trail, grown cold during her long confinement in hospital and convalescence. Meticulously she began pulling together all the loose strings she could find. She interviewed survivors, regional drug dealers, prison inmates, people with intelligence connections who would talk—anyone who might shed light on the bombing. More and more it looked as though it was an attempt to do away with Pastora, and lay the blame on the Sandanistas.

Morgan and her film crew failed to find a smoking gun. Too many years had elapsed. But they did determine that the terrorist bomber was a hired Libyan hit man who had entered and left Nicaragua under journalistic cover. But hired by whom? Every significant lead Morgan uncovered inevitably pointed to the CIA, where of course she was met with a cold wall of indifference and silence.

In her own mind, Morgan felt certain the job had been sponsored by American intelligence. It is a conclusion Eden Pastora agrees with completely.

vvv

The callous use of reporters as common cannon fodder when it serves the sinister purposes of intelligence agencies unfortunately helps to fuel the outright cynicism that over time seeps into the journalistic profession.

The La Penca incident certainly points up the need for journalists themselves to be more vigilant of the credentials and trustworthiness of travelling companions during dangerous assignments. After his brush with death, Torgensen, the Swedish TV cameraman who befriended the terrorist, summed up his feelings with this understatement: "In future I'll make sure of new friends. This incident has changed my perception of people."

Generally speaking, spies don't make good news reporters and journalists don't make good spies.

Vivid proof of the latter is the tragic case of Farzad Bazoft, an Iranian-British journalist. Bazoft wasn't a professional intelligence agent masquerading as a reporter, but a reporter moonlighting as a spy.*

Iran-born and British-based, the 31-year-old reporter for London's *The Observer* was convicted by an Iraqi court of spying for Britain and Israel and hanged in 1990. He had been arrested six months earlier while working on an investigative story for his paper.

Bazoft, and a 52-year-old British nurse, were apprehended while checking reports of a massive explosion and fire at the highly secret and heavily guarded Al-Iskandria military research complex outside Baghdad. Bazoft was disguised as an Indian doctor, and the two travelled to the site in an ambulance.

One of the accusations made against Bazoft in court was that he scooped up soil samples at the complex. These, it was alleged, were to be analyzed for chemical content.

The Observer vehemently denied that Bazoft was engaged in espionage for the British, the Israelis, or anyone else. It probably did so in good faith because British intelligence wouldn't necessarily inform *The Observer* that it had one of its reporters on the newspaper's payroll. (Although there have been cases where news organizations have co-operated fully with intelligence agencies.)

When a journalist becomes enmeshed in an espionage scandal no one is more surprised nor quicker to vouch for the reporter's innocence than his journalistic colleagues. In a profession where stories are approached with a healthy skepticism tinged with cynicism, it is surprising that

---

* Bazoft was friend and schoolmate of the author's youngest son during a European posting.

vvv

journalists are loath to believe that one of their own may be packing a cloak and dagger along with the lap top word processor.

In a letter to the *Globe & Mail* John Fraser, one of Canada's highly regarded journalists and former foreign correspondent, stated flatly that, "I do not believe for a moment that Mr. Bazoft was a spy—for Israel, or Great Britain, or any other country. He had a classic journalist's inability to hold onto a secret, much preferring to see any such information in type with his by-line on top of it."

Fraser tells of socializing with Bazoft, "a charming and ambitious young journalist who lived on the fringes of real poverty and was eager for any freelance writing or research projects he could pick up."

It was generally known in the London Foreign Press club that Bazoft had a brush with the law soon after his escape to Britain from revolution-crazed Iran. Penniless and jobless, he was found guilty of robbing a savings and loan office of 900 dollars and threatening to blow up the building.

With 20-20 hindsight fellow journalists might have concluded, in Bazoft's case, that the ingredients for being co-opted into espionage were all there. The ambitious young reporter had journalistic cover with a quality British paper, he desperately needed money, he was keen on research, wanted to cover-up a criminal past and, perhaps most important and useful of all, he had a Middle East background.

Several weeks after Bazoft's execution, and more stout denials from his newspaper and fellow reporters, British intelligence confirmed that Bazoft had indeed been on their payroll but denied that he was working for them on the Iraqi assignment.

If Bazoft was indeed pursuing what he saw as a legitimate story, he broke every rule in the book. And so did his employer.

The first rule for any reporter, especially on foreign assignment, is never to pretend to be anything but a professional journalist. It is possible, just possible, that Bazoft may have been spared the noose if he had entered the forbidden military zone simply as a journalist and not in disguise. Pursuing that kind of story in a country where compassion is regarded as weakness carried a high risk as it was. Trying to get the story under the pretext of being a doctor driving an ambulance sealed Bazoft's fate.

Clearly, he was the wrong person to assign to the wrong story at the wrong place at the most inappropriate time. The Iranian-born journalist arrived in Baghdad with the Iran-Iraq war, with its horrific death toll still seared in every Iraqi's mind. It was also no secret that Iraq was engaged in manufacturing lethal biological weapons and was working feverishly to build its own nuclear attack capability. (In 1981, Israeli jets knocked out Baghdad's fledgling nuclear research reactor.)

vvv

The Bazoft case had a chilling effect on journalists assigned to Baghdad. Bernard Shaw of CNN says when he packed his bags for an assignment in Iraq just before the Gulf War broke out, he tossed in his binoculars as he'd always done on foreign jobs. "Then," he says, "I thought better of it. With the Bazoft execution fresh in my mind I took those binoculars out of my suitcase." Says ABC's Peter Jennings, "the most frightening thing in this business is an accusation that you're a spy."

Bob Simon and his CBS crew had just such a life-and-death experience during the 1991 Gulf War. Simon, like hundreds of other reporters, had been roaming around the International Hotel at Dhahran Saudi Arabia reading pooled reports written by his peers. He sat in at the carefully-packaged daily military briefings. Chafing under these restrictions he, CBS's London bureau chief Peter Bluff, freelance cameraman Roberto Alvarez and soundman Juan Caldera took off on their own heading toward Iraqi lines along the Kuwait border. There, sitting in the sand, their abandoned vehicle was found. It contained equipment, money, personal effects—but the four newsmen were nowhere to be seen.

Three weeks later, it was learned that travelling unsupervised, they had been captured by Iraqi forces near the Kuwaiti-Saudi border and taken to Baghdad to be interrogated as spies.

Simon says all four were blindfolded and beaten and questioned at the same time. "When they were getting to important questions," says Simon, "they opened the door and beat Juan, Peter and Roberto so they would scream while they were asking me questions and beating me at the same time." They were threatened daily with execution for espionage.

At one point, allied bombs hit the military intelligence headquarters where they were being held. "That was the scariest moment," says Alvarez. A bomb smashed through the roof, sending masonry flying through his room. He survived with nothing more serious than an injured ankle.

After prodding from Soviet president Mikhail Gorbachev, the Iraqis released the CBS crew. They had been held in awful circumstances for 40 days. They had lost weight because of malnutrition, but otherwise were in fairly good shape. They were luckier than Farzod Bazoft.

These cases underline the point that nowhere are foreign correspondents obliged to pick their way through political mine fields with greater care than in the Middle East.

The scene is Iran at the height of that country's war with Iraq. A bus is rumbling toward a high-security military airport with its cargo of Western reporters returning from the front where they've witnessed heavy Iranian artillery in action. The shelling has given one member of the group a pounding headache.

vvv

A British reporter offers his colleague an aspirin. Suddenly a look of cold fear crosses his face. The tablets are made in Israel with Hebraic printing on the box. In Iran that could have serious consequences. The Ayatolla's Revolutionary Guard consider Israel an enemy second only to the great American Satan himself. If crossed, the zealous guards may detain as a spy any reporter who has been to Israel.

It is for this reason that correspondents who cover Israel as well as Iran and the Arab States go through their luggage with a fine toothed comb before venturing out of Israel. Store tags are removed from clothing, stamps discarded, pockets purged of shekels and–a top priority—passports are freed from any Israeli markings. The offending box of aspirin escaped the reporter's scrutiny. Given the background of paranoia in Iran, his anxiety is understandable as the bus approaches the airport security gate. All goes well, and under the cover of darkness the offending box is quietly flipped out the window. Its discovery the next morning is certain to give a headache of a different sort to a baffled military police.

Covering both sides of a conflict can be a dangerous game. Charges of espionage by one side or the other are almost inevitable.

In 1948 the body of a 34 year old CBS correspondent, George Polk, washed up on a beach in Greece. He had been bound hand and foot. There was a neat bullet hole in the back of his head.

Polk had been covering the Greek civil war. Not satisfied with the self-serving government handouts, he decided to report from the communist guerilla hideouts as well. He pulled no punches and fearlessly reported the dishonesty and corruption of the U.S.-supported Royalist government.

To this day there is no proof that the Greek government was responsible for Polk's murder. What is known is that the government tried to frame the communist insurgents and got the complete co-operation of American intelligence in doing so. Washington was more concerned with the rising postwar communist menace than it was in solving the murder of a reporter, even if he was one of their own.

Polk, a decorated WW II navy pilot turned journalist became one of the first, but by no means the last, of the cold war expendables.

As the embarrassing witnesses to graft, corruption, torture, officially-sanctioned murder, aggression and a myriad of other crimes committed by governments and their officials, journalists face daily physical danger in wars, civil conflict and violent demonstrations. High-profile television crews are especially at risk. To silence testimony of these witnesses, totalitarian governments will continue to label them as spies whenever it suits their purpose. The fact that some espionage operatives do pass themselves off as reporters gives a degree of legitimacy to these charges.

vv

In many cases it is simply an inability on the part of the police and military to differentiate between news and intelligence information.

Given this situation, the International Press Institute warns employers to claim a reporter immediately after he or she is reported missing. Failure to do so reinforces the suspicion of espionage.

Bob Simon credits his employer with saving his life and the lives of his crew by immediately sounding the alarm and claiming them as CBS journalists.

Making contact with a journalist's captors, however, isn't always easy. Jon Swain, a reporter for the *The Times* of London, was kidnapped in Ethiopia and held for three months. Tigray People's Liberation forces didn't release him until they finally heard the BBC report that he really was a journalist.

There is much journalists themselves can do to avoid being mistaken for intelligence agents. When in a war zone, especially in Third World countries, reporters should avoid as much of the usual journalistic gear and gadgetry as possible. It's to no avail trying to convince some uneducated border guard that all the sophisticated technical paraphernalia you're packing is really required for your job. Nor does it do any good pointing out to him that a real spy wouldn't be that obvious.

David Zucchino of the *Philadelphia Enquirer* relates a story of just how far espionage paranoia can go in some countries. Writing in *Journalists on Dangerous Assignments: A Guide for Staying Alive,* he tells of a photographer in Lebanon whipping out his state-of-the-art light meter. The dial spelled out f-16, the f-stop. A Druse militiaman read it and started screaming abuse at the photographer, accusing him of calling in an Israeli air strike. (The Israelis fly F-16 jets.)

The key to defusing situations like this (or avoiding them in the first place) is to be totally open and frank about equipment being used. It should be explained to anyone who is curious and they should be encouraged to try it out. Small favors should be offered whenever possible and in almost any tight situation politeness works wonders.

Carrying maps, especially circling or marking destinations and routes can lead to no end of trouble. It may be nothing more than a road map, but to an illiterate kid packing an AK-47, it can look awfully suspicious.

The locale is Zimbabwe's Matabeleland. An American and Canadian reporter pull up at a roadblock on a dusty bush road, manned by the notorious Fifth Brigade, an outfit with the reputation for shooting first and not asking questions later. The troops have just burned a nearby village to the ground and are in a foul mood. Nevertheless everything goes smoothly during the car search, until some maps are discovered. The soldiers don't seem to know, or care to know, that strangers would get

vvv

hopelessly lost in the bush without them, or that the maps were printed and sold by the Zimbabwe government. The reporters are accused of being spies and spend several nerve-wracking hours contemplating their fate before being released.

It might be assumed that glasnost, first introduced by the old Soviet Union, will reduce the need for East-West espionage activities. Experts don't agree. Oleg Gordievsky, KGB station chief in London before his defection in 1985, predicts an expansion of spying activity by Russia as the country attempts to rebuild. The emphasis, he told *Time* magazine, will probably shift slightly toward industrial intelligence. George Carver, a former high-ranking CIA official, also dismisses any easing of intelligence requirements as super power rivalry declines. "The cold war may be ending," he says, "but there is no detente in the intelligence war." U.S. Senator David L. Boren, chairman of the Senate Select Committee on Intelligence, takes a similar view. Writing in the *New York Times*, he notes that, "the fastest growing area of espionage activities by foreign governments against the United States is not theft of military secrets, but theft of commercial secrets from private American companies to further national economic interests." According to the Senator, the same applies to all other developed industrial countries.

So, while the old Soviet military threat has receded, it is rapidly being replaced by a proliferation of chemical, biological and nuclear weapons in the Third World. It is this area, especially the Middle East, that presents the greatest danger to world stability. Given this situation, journalism will continue to be the target of intelligence exploitation. Intelligence will continue to pay reporters for information and infiltrate the profession by getting jobs or freelance assignments for their agents. The lure of money and the perceived glamor of the spy business will continue to prove irresistible for some reporters. There are also those who become involved involuntarily. Journalists who work in states which control both the media and the intelligence agency are particularly vulnerable. They can be easily intimidated and coerced. A professional code of ethics under such circumstances is often practically useless.

Reporters assigned to volatile hot spots, especially in the Third World, must be constantly aware that totally different conceptions of the journalist's role prevail. What is considered normal reporting in one country may be seen as espionage in another.

The Manipulators

There are really only three ways to deal with the press: The best way is to tell them everything. This keeps them busy and eventually exhausts and bores them. The next best way is to tell them nothing, which at least excites the cop in them and gives them the excitement of a mystery. The worst way .... is to try to manipulate them, to pretend to be candid in private conversation, but to use every trick in the book to get them to fill the headlines and front pages with calculated trash.

— James Reston

"I'M READY AND PREPARED FOR DIRECT DIALOGUE BEtween me, President Bush and Mrs. Thatcher." That's Iraqi president Saddam Hussein speaking on the eve of the Gulf War. He's not on the phone to his foreign minister, or sending a message to his ambassadors in Washington and London, he's on American television speaking to Dan Rather of CBS news. A few days before Atlanta-based CNN (Cable Network News) showed in its entirety Hussein's television appearance with Western hostages. Patting the heads of children and speaking soothingly to the others, he tried to create a public image of a benevolent peace-loving fatherly figure. It may have worked at home but his efforts to win hearts and minds in the West fell flat.

In both cases the Iraqi strongman by-passed normal diplomatic channels to try to influence directly international public opinion (CNN is now seen in 95 countries around the world.) Media analysts describe this phenomenon as electronic diplomacy or the democratization of international relations.

It is interesting to conjecture how Nikita Khruschev would have played his hand if he had held the instant diplomacy card during the Cuban missile crisis. Would he have by-passed the United Nations and gone over to CNN to bang his shoe on live television? As the world teetered on the brink of nuclear war in that autumn of 1962, would the showman Soviet leader have chosen to ignore normal diplomatic channels in favor of live television dialogue with Washington?

As it was, the impulsive Khruschev sent Kennedy two telegrams almost simultaneously. One was belligerent, the other conciliatory. Kennedy had time to make a deliberate choice as to which one he would reply to. As we know, he chose the conciliatory one, thus defusing a potential Armageddon.

vv

Television has gone beyond being an observer of events to becoming a player. Participatory, or "street TV," became the catalyst of an unstoppable democratic force in Eastern Europe in the late eighties. As totalitarian regimes lost the technological battle to keep out foreign TV signals and ultimately were denied a monopoly on domestic television to advance their own agenda, they toppled like so many dominos. The infection of democracy spread from country to country carried by television pictures of freedom marches, demonstrations and the dismantling of walls and border watch towers. Border guards were powerless to keep out ideas. Television was like oxygen feeding an exploding conflagration. Electronic diplomacy was launched on its dizzying course forever changing the structure of international relations.

Media guru Marshall McLuhan saw it all coming 25 years ago, when he wrote: "As the speed of information increases, the tendency is for policies to move away from representation and delegation of constituents toward immediate involvement of the entire community in the central acts of decision." Live television is involving all of us in the national and global decision making process, sometimes with tragic consequences.

The TV reports on student protests in Korea and the Philippines made China's students think they too could force immediate government change. It resulted in a bloody massacre and a sharp reversal of the liberating process.

Indeed, television is bringing us the event before it happens. Through television, the Iraqis told us directly that we were doomed. Americans calculated casualties in advance and took the necessary precautions through a protracted air war to minimize them. Lance Morrow of *Time* magazine says reality of wars has lost its cause, effect and dramatic pace. "The natural rhythms of war making have gone electronic . . . . time gets dismantled somehow . . . . the adrenalin rushes prematurely; the cost gets reckoned before the development."

It has become accepted practice for governments and movements to use the media whenever and wherever they can to promote their interests. Television in particular has been recognized for the powerful tool it is, and is being used, if not as a total replacement for conventional diplomacy, certainly as a powerful alternative.

TV cuts to the very heart of the matter to speed up the diplomatic process. Nevertheless, once both sides have reached the point of being serious about resolving an issue and playing to the masses has served its purpose, the cameras are as assiduously spurned as they once were courted.

When war broke out in the Persian Gulf between the American-led coalition forces and Iraq, only CNN was allowed to continue to operate

vvv

in Baghdad. Having served their purpose, everyone else was kicked out. Baghdad's official explanation was that it was the only Western news service that was objective and impartial. Such a compliment from one of the belligerents was something of an embarrassment for the world's only global news service which is watched by heads of state all over the world. CNN had been used for months before the war as a conduit for unofficial information Washington wanted Baghdad to hear, and information the Iraqis wished to transmit to Washington. CNN had to choose between maintaining its news service, knowing they were subject to manipulation by the Iraqis, or shut down. CNN chose to stay. In doing so, history was made. For the first time reporters from a belligerent nation covered the enemy camp.

The Allies manipulated the media far more skilfully and blatantly than the Iraqis. So skilfully in fact that information reaching the folks back home was often little more that carefully orchestrated propaganda. It was coverage of the world's first sanitized war. Instead of pictures of people being blown to bits, we saw dramatic telephoto video shots of bombs being lobbed through ventilating shafts and taking out bridge spans seconds after a motorist sped through the crosshairs.

Correspondents, instead of being out in the field, got a daily diet of filtered briefings by generals in polished boots and carefully pressed combat fatigues. The long awaited ground attack took a mere 100 hours to bring the war to an end with little opportunity for correspondents to see anything.

Next stop, home for the celebrations and victory parades. It all had a surrealistic air about it. The war was so neatly packaged and meticulously choreographed that no one would have suspected that in a little more than 40 days, perhaps as many as 100 000 Iraqis died—least of all the correspondents who covered it and the public which they tried to inform.

The war over, reporters were again free to roam at will with camera, pen and pad. They went north where they discovered that the fighting wasn't over after all. There the Kurds were rebelling against Saddam Hussein, and Baghdad's Republican Guard was systematically slaughtering them. For the first time during the war, reporters told the story the way it was unfolding—hundreds of thousands of Kurds, many women, some carrying newborn infants, and men and children fleeing through treacherous mountain passes to escape extermination.

Once correspondents were allowed to reenter the real world the pictures were no longer pretty. No more long distance aerial shots of bridges going up in puffs of black smoke, no more self-important generals strutting beside neatly colored maps and charts. These scenes were replaced with those of bare, bleeding feet tramping through a sea of mud;

vv

of children with skin blistered by napalm; of dead babies wrapped in rags and buried under rock piles.

The speed and efficiency with which news moves between world capitals is having a direct impact on diplomatic missions and their relationships with the press. The day when an ambassador was the sole eyes and ears of his government is over. Much of the same information embassies gather is more rapidly available in the morning papers and on the news broadcasts. This fact prompted Pierre Trudeau to suggest that modern communications had made expensive embassies around the world redundant. The comment (probably intended to needle his external affairs department) wasn't taken seriously, but it did underline the self-assumed role of the media as the essential conduit of day to day information on events and developments abroad—even for governments.

Most ambassadors have recognized this fact of life and try to use it to their advantage by maintaining regular contact with their country's correspondents in their assigned capitals. A few still try to maintain a see-all, know-all facade. Canadian correspondent John Fraser, in his book *The Chinese,* recounts how the French ambassador in Beijing took it as a personal affront if Paris ever got political information from news reports before it had been filed by his own staff. His frazzled officers were obliged to hang around the news agencies to find out what was about to be filed and rush back to brief their ambassador who would then presumably try to get his dispatches to Paris first.

Other embassies, including the British, American and Canadian, also use overseas journalists as sources of information, but do so in a more open manner. Many ambassadors hold regular group meetings with their national correspondents where such information either side wishes to divulge is exchanged in an informal and casual way. It is of course, a subtle attempt on the part of the embassies to influence the reporters in not straying too far from the official line being fed back to their governments.

There are also minor pluses for reporters in these exchanges—being told about visits by VIPs, trade or cultural delegations and so on. Anything of major consequence is, however, seldom if ever revealed by either side. An ambassador is not about to reveal information to reporters before he sends it to his government and reporters aren't about to scoop themselves either—especially in the presence of their competitors.

At times, attempts at manipulation by embassies can be somewhat heavy-handed, as illustrated by my Moscow diary notes of February 17, 1969.

vv

> H.M. from Canadian embassy called this a.m. informed me that
> as press officer he had an interest in my reports. Explained that
> in a country like U.S.S.R., government assumes what is aired on
> CBC is Canadian policy. To avoid misunderstanding and political
> embarrassment with Soviets, it would be advisable if I "dis-
> cussed" my reports with him before hand. Told him I couldn't
> think of a faster way of being fired than agreeing to something
> like that. Our people seem just as ignorant about what constitutes
> a free and independent press as the Soviets.

An even more ham-handed attempt at press control by a Canadian
foreign officer happened in Helsinki several months later. The following
is from my notes while on assignment covering the U.S.-Soviet SALT I
disarmament talks in the Finnish capital in the fall of 1969.

> Mr. T. called from our embassy few minutes after checking into
> Vaacuna Hotel. Wanted to get together for dinner. Asked what I
> was doing in Helsinki, which I suggested should be obvious; first
> phase of Strategic Arms Limitation Talks scheduled to start day
> after tomorrow. Told him I'd be doing a few scene setters—pre-
> carious Finnish political situation balancing East-West cold war
> tight rope etc. Mr. T. informed me Canada engaged in delicate
> trade negotiations with the Finns regarding possible sale of Candu
> reactor and advised me not to say anything in my reports that
> might jeopardize these negotiations. Lost my cool. Told him
> bluntly to mind his own business. (Good God, what nasty things
> can you say about the inoffensive Finns?) Needless to say, dinner
> ended on a sour note—and it wasn't the Finnish cloud berry
> dessert.

On the rare occasion when diplomats do slip into candor, and say things
they wouldn't want included in the diplomatic pouch mailed home, they
go to any lengths to keep it from being made public—threaten, deny,
plead no-attribution—even beg. Usually the plea is that everything was
off the record—even if it wasn't.

Peter Worthington experienced such a lapse of diplomatic protocol
during an interview with J.J. Hurley, Canadian ambassador to South
Africa during the Diefenbaker administration. Hurley made it abundantly
clear that his views on apartheid were diametrically opposed to those of
the Canadian government he represented—a government that had just
spearheaded the ouster of South Africa from the Commonwealth. He was
fulsome in his praise of the Nationalist government and the advantages
to blacks under what he perceived as a benevolent policy of apartheid.

Worthington couldn't wait to file his "bombshell." Realizing he'd gone
too far, Hurley insisted everything had been off the record. Worthington
insisted just as vehemently that it had been on the record. The ambassador

vv

was reduced to pleading: "Please, I'm asking you. It was meant for off the record. Do you want to destroy me? I am due to retire this year. Whatever you write will be misunderstood."

Worthington agonized. What purpose would such a one-day sensation really serve? Was it worth destroying the reputation of a decorated war hero and distinguished diplomat?

In the end he didn't write the story. To this day, he isn't sure whether he did the right thing. It's the kind of dilemma every journalist had to deal with at one time or another. It's a problem that is perhaps easier for foreign-based reporters. The consequences of withholding a foreign story usually carry less impact than one of national significance. The Hurley case represents succumbing to manipulation aimed at the very heart of a human being's compassion for his fellow man—a quality not entirely lacking even in journalists.

Time magazine's Strobe Talbot has no regrets today about killing a story he obtained under similar circumstances during the chilliest period of the Cold War. Long before Gorbachev's perestroika and glasnost, Bulgaria's 34-year-old Deputy Minister of Trade, Andrei Lukanov, did the unthinkable—thinking out loud. The ambitious but honest communist apparatchik levelled with Talbot. He confessed that some kind of synthesis or coming together of Marxism and a market economy was essential if communist countries were to extricate themselves from the mess they were in. Heresy at the time.

Then *Time* decided to do an article on "bright young faces" in European politics, Talbot dug out his interview with Lukanov. It was an honor the young minister wanted to be spared at all costs. Such a splash in the capitalist press would have ended Lukanov's promising career then and there.

He sent an emissary to Talbot's home. "Please, the interview was unofficial and done in good faith." (A Marxist version of off the record.)

Talbot killed the story, reasoning that journalists too are subject to their own version of a principle of physics—by observing (and reporting) a phenomenon, it may be altered, perhaps to the detriment of those who co-operated with the reporter.

Eighteen years later, in a free and open election, the Bulgarian people ousted the communist old guard and chose Lukanov as their prime minister. If Talbot had not spiked his story, would Lukanov have been around to run for elected office and effect a badly needed economic reform in his country? (Lukanov resigned six months later because of wide spread opposition to his government's austerity program.)

It is a rare reporter indeed who can say he or she has never "covered" for anyone. It's not done as readily today as it once was, but it is still done.

vv

Putting a story under wraps can mean keeping sources intact, remaining on a first name basis with people in high places, special invitations and being rewarded with exclusive high level interviews. This carrot and stick approach to manipulation is practised everywhere, in non-democratic states and in democracies.

Few forms of manipulation make the reporter as uncomfortable as the you're-one-of-us kind. This type of media control is most prevalent in national political reporting and attempts to exploit the reporter's race, religion, ethnic and regional origins. Dan Rather's experiences with President Lyndon Johnson, well known among journalists at the time and detailed in David Halberstam's book, *The Powers That Be* illustrate just how shamelessly the president tried to exploit their Texas connection.

Johnson welcomed Rather's appointment to cover the White House.* "You're a fellow Texan," he would say, "you're not one of those Eastern bastards, you understand me. You're going to help me and I can help you." As Halberstam points out, the rancher president liked to put his brand on people but Rather wasn't easily branded. He refused to play the game and persisted in doing reports criticizing the president. Being a maverick in Johnson's media entourage carried a price and Rather paid it. In the president's eyes, Rather became a non person—invisible.

Try as he might the White House reporter of the country's mightiest broadcasting network consistently tried to catch the President's eye at news conferences, but to no avail. American newspaper reporters can survive without being seen asking the President questions. For a reporter from a major television network it's a career-shattering blow. Being on the outs with the President can mean trouble with superiors at head office.

Rather was in trouble and he knew it. He contacted Jack Valenti, White House confidant, friend of reporters, and all-round nice guy and unburdened himself. Valenti soothed Rather's ruffled feathers, assuring him that Johnson really liked Rather—but the President had that pesky problem of poor eyesight. He'd been looking for Rather, but just couldn't find him in that news conference crowd.

The other network reporters? Oh, they were just a blur too, but he knew them by their shapes and outlines. At the next conference, Rather was recognized. Apparently Johnson had either boned up on the CBS reporter's silhouette or his eyesight had magically improved.

But Rather's days at the White House were numbered. Johnson complained constantly to the CBS executives about the flinty reporter's work.

---

* With a Texan in the White House, CBS thought it would be good politics to have someone with a Texas accent cover him.

vv

In the end, CBS transferred him to another beat. The Texas connection hadn't worked. Rather was, as Johnson saw it, a Texan good ol' boy gone bad, corrupted by "those Eastern people."

John Diefenbaker was like that too. A prairie lawyer turned politician, he had an abiding distrust of Easterners or the "Bay Street boys" as he called them. And, he expected prairie people to stick together.

Diefenbaker was prime minister when I came to Ottawa in 1962 as CTV Parliamentary reporter, and it was primarily because of my own Western origins that I got the job. In the summer of that year the fledgling television web was assembling a news team in preparation for the inauguration of its first nightly national newscasts originating in Ottawa.

Peter Jennings and Baden Langton had been taken on fairly early in the talent hunt. Both were from Ontario. Stu Griffiths, manager of the originating station CJOH, was as politically savvy as he was knowledgeable about broadcasters. He realized that the team needed a Western counterbalance. He knew that bringing a Westerner on board would win him points with CTV stations in Winnipeg, Edmonton, Calgary and Vancouver, each of which had a considerable financial stake in the new network. But there was another reason why I was picked. (Besides the fact that I thought I was a pretty good reporter.) Stu rationalized that a Westerner would have easier access to the prime minister's office—and as usual Stu was right.

I had barely found my way through the cavernous Centre Block to the press gallery washroom before I, as a fellow-Albertan, began getting invitations to Alberta Conservative caucus lunches. Nothing was ever said, but the implications were clear that if I helped the Tories, they were definitely in a position to help me make a national name for myself. And, the Alberta contingent under Diefenbaker wasn't without clout. Calgary's Douglas Harkness was the Minister of National Defence, and Marcel Lambert from Edmonton was soon to become Speaker of the House of Commons. Both men, particularly Harkness, gave me generous access even though television news was still relatively new, and politicians did not agree as readily to televised interviews as they do today. In a short time, the prime minister too cleared his schedule for an interview practically on request. (Diefenbaker invariably made time for any reporter he liked.)

Interviews with Diefenbaker were rarely rushed. He was particularly expansive with fellow-Westerners, who he seemed to assume were on his side in his struggle against vaguely-defined dark forces simply referred to as "they." "They told me it couldn't be done." "They opposed me on that," and so on.

vvv

After my first interview with Diefenbaker, he gave me a "tour" of his office, pointing out autographed photographs of various heads of state, including one of the Queen. "Over here," pointing to a particular wall panel, "this is where Sir John A. MacDonald had his secret door, so he could slip in and out of his office unseen after he'd had a few."

Like a pensioner killing time, the prime minister reminisced about his days as a teacher in a one-room Saskatchewan school house, about shooting gophers in the schoolyard with his older students and getting caught by the inspector. He pulled yellowing photographs from under a huge green blotter that covered the biggest part of his neat desk. One was of the sod shack, built by his parents who had come from Ontario to homestead in Saskatchewan; another of himself as a young lieutenant in a WW I uniform.

After delivering a brief commentary, he deposited each photo carefully beside a bright red telephone that dominated his desk. It was the hot line between Ottawa and Washington on which, Diefenbaker was fond of telling his visitors,"I can get Ike any time I want to."

If there were any pressing matters of state demanding the Canadian prime minister's attention on that sunny autumn day, they would have to wait. John Diefenbaker was in an expansive mood reliving his days as a prairie farm boy, school teacher and lawyer. He was in the company of a Westerner who cared and understood, a reporter whose sympathy and support he felt he could count on. The prime minister would soon need all the support he could muster. Discontent over his leadership was already brewing in the Conservative ranks while the party was in power; it broke into full rebellion after Diefenbaker's defeat in 1963 and the Tories return to the Opposition benches.

Those who demonstrated total loyalty to the Chief were known on the Hill as Diefenbaker's cowboys. Among the most loyal was the Alberta wing of the Tory caucus. (With the exception of Douglas Harkness, who had resigned from the cabinet over defense policy before the election.) The Alberta caucus prided itself on being Diefenbaker stalwarts and included among its membership the rough and ready Horner brothers, Hugh & Jack, who were always eager to head up a posse to hunt down any renegade who had it in for the Chief.

When hints of doubt about Diefenbaker's ability to lead began to surface within this diehard group, I wrote the story—and promptly landed in hot water.

Marcel Lambert, MP from Edmonton West, phoned me the morning after my report had aired. His voice fairly shaking with anger, he accused me of fabricating the whole thing, and then more in sorrow than anger,

vv

told me how disappointed he was in the performance of a fellow Edmontonian of whom until now he had the highest professional regard.

Diefenbaker was equally livid. When I encountered him in a hallway a few days after my report, he admonished me as though I were an errant school boy. "You've allowed yourself to be taken in by them—I'm disappointed in you." It would be a long time before I enjoyed the easy access to his office I once had.

Diefenbaker was also to be deeply disappointed by his own "cowboys." One by one they slipped away from his beleaguered encampment—including Marcel Lambert. Only a handful led by the Horners rode with the Chief to the end of the road at Maple Leaf Gardens in Toronto where he was ignominiously defeated at the 1967 leadership convention.

Once crossed Diefenbaker could hold a grudge for life. In my case it didn't last that long. In the 1968 election he wasn't campaigning as prime minister, nor as leader of the Conservative party. He was John Diefenbaker, lowly MP for Prince Albert and nothing more. Few reporters paid any attention to him. I thought he was still a good story and took my CBC television crew to Saskatchewan to pick up his election campaign tour. We met him on the grounds of a school in Nipawin where he landed by helicopter. There was no one from the media with him, and I was the only national reporter to meet him on his arrival. He didn't say anything, but his blue eyes sparkled and I knew he was delighted to see us. For me, it was the story of a once great actor returning to a familiar stage as a bit player. For Diefenbaker, I sensed it was vindication that the corrosive influence of the Eastern media might have damaged me but that my basic Western loyalty was intact.

The next time our paths crossed was in Moscow. As an ordinary MP with no leadership responsibility Diefenbaker had time on his hands and decided to do some travelling. He wasn't entirely welcome in the Soviet Union. Whether in his capacity as prime minister, leader of the opposition, or MP, he had consistently supported independence for the Ukraine and the Baltics. His concern for the people of these captive Soviet republics was no doubt sincere, but championing their cause also meant votes from Canada's large Ukrainian, Lithuanian, Estonian and Latvian communities.

"Well Ab, it isn't Nipawin, Saskatchewan, is it?" were his first words when I called at his room at the National Hotel, the domes of the Kremlin clearly visible from his window.

Diefenbaker, as a visitor who was stripped of political power, with little chance of ever regaining it, was given low priority by the Russians. They did, however, provide limousine service during his visit to the Ukraine where he instructed his hosts to scour the countryside for what he

vvv

described as a typical Ukrainian village like the ones he had seen in Saskatchewan. His Soviet hosts insisted that there weren't any—that rural people all lived in modern apartments on collective farms such as we had just visited. Dief would have none of that. Soon our small convoy of black limos was churning up clouds of dust on a summer fallow field as we headed toward the depths of the Ukrainian hinterland.

Diefenbaker got to see his Ukrainian village complete with the traditional long-poled well. He joked in his limited Ukrainian vocabulary with kerchiefed women working the small private garden plots that ringed their thatched whitewashed cottages with dirt floors. For Dief it was a small triumph. The Soviets might be able to bamboozle some visitors—but not him.

More of the same was to follow the next morning in Kiev during a visit with officials at the Ukrainian Parliament. The meeting did not go well. Free of the diplomatic niceties government leaders are obliged to respect regardless of circumstances, Diefenbaker gave the Soviets a piece of his mind. He stormed out of the building straight past his waiting limousine, across the street and into the rented Volga sedan I was sharing with Jack Cahill of the *Toronto Star*. He harrumphed that he was not about to swallow the communist line he'd just been fed and suggested we leave. "Where to, Mr. Diefenbaker?" I asked. "Oh, anywhere," he replied, "anywhere at all." I headed in the general direction of his hotel, with the perplexed limo driver in hot pursuit, obviously puzzled by the strange behavior of his charge from Canada.

It wouldn't be the last time a visiting Canadian politician would throw a monkey wrench into the well-laid transportation plans of their Soviet hosts. A year later Pierre Trudeau, then prime minister, visited the USSR. He had just ended a meeting with the Soviet leader Leonid Brehznev and was walking towards his limousine, flanked by a four-man police motorcycle escort. On an impulse, Trudeau jumped on one of the motorcycles and took off around the cobblestone Kremlin courtyard, the startled motorcycle cop giving chase on foot.

The art of media manipulators is honed to near perfection during election campaigns in both the United States and Canada. All major parties and candidates hire media experts, often ex-journalists who have evolved as power brokers of the political system. And, if the truth be known, journalists willingly jump into bed with these fellows.

Larry Sabato, associate professor of government and foreign affairs at the University of Virginia, has charged that these consultants are in the business of deceiving the public and journalists.

A "sweetheart arrangement" is what Sabato calls the relationship between the consultants and the press. Sabato accuses journalists of using

vvv

consultants as permanent sources, during and in-between election campaigns. "You need the information they provide," he tells journalists "so you're inclined to treat them rather nicely . . . . and they're almost never criticized."

As a result of this pseudo incestuous relationship, critics allege few stories critical of political consultants are ever written.

These sweetheart deals with politicians and their advisers reach their apogee during election campaigns. Political leaders in every country where free elections are allowed pander shamelessly to the needs of journalism, television in particular. Each day the leadership candidate's schedule is geared to one single goal—making the lead story on the evening television news, and given television's penchant for the dramatic and pictorial, style and human interest inevitably win over substance.

The practice, like so many trends in journalism, originated in the United States specifically during the 1968 presidential campaign. It is now firmly entrenched in countries like Canada and the United Kingdom. "Each day," Nixon wrote in one of his memoirs, "we wanted to do everything we could to influence what that night's network lead would be."

As might be expected, no one played the game more superbly than Hollywood actor turned presidential candidate, Ronald Reagan. His successor George Bush proved to be a quick study, as did Brian Mulroney in Canada. Their successors will prove to be no exception.

As a result, during election campaigns, political leaders and their advisers not only decide what the story will be, where it will take place and when it occurs, but also largely determine how it will be written and where it will run on the evening news.

Media reaction is schizophrenic. On the one hand journalists feel prostituted and used. On the other hand they are hooked on the practice and quite like it.

Political reporters have an in-born herding instinct. Any candidate who departs from the topic-a-day syndrome by injecting more than one issue into a speech, risks being criticized by the press for conducting an aimless and unfocused campaign. If the truth were known, it is the reporters who are confused. If the lead isn't made obviously apparent, there is a lot of whispering and schmoozing on the campaign plane in a desperate effort to reach a consensus on what to go with. And woe unto the independent thinking maverick whose lead differs from that of the pack. He or she will have a lot of explaining to do at the editor's desk.

It is all so much easier and safer when the candidates themselves dictate what the lead story for each day will be—Monday it's the environment,

vvv

Tuesday, the cost of social services, Wednesday, defense cuts—and so on.

All this, of course, assumes that issues are dealt with at all, with politicians refraining from taking cheap shots at opponents and reporters not indulging in a diet of personality profiles and sensationalism.

The media have a clear responsibility not simply to "follow" the leaders on the campaign trail but also to define the issues when candidates fail to do so.

The 1988 Canadian general election is a case in point. There were two crucial issues facing Canadians at that time, the Goods and Services Tax and free trade with the U.S. Only free trade was dealt with by the politicians, so subsequently it was the only issue taken up by the media. The GST remained a silent issue throughout the campaign. The opposition parties raised it in a half-hearted manner from time to time, but the media remained totally oblivious to a barely camouflaged tax proposal which would have sweeping political and economic ramifications for the country. Not until the Conservatives were swept back into power and the unpopular tax introduced did the media realize what a time bomb it was. By then it was too late to engage the public in debate. The people had no choice but to accept an unpopular tax which they had not expected and knew little about.

The public was short-changed on the free trade issue as well. It was, in contrast to the GST, hotly debated but that debate produced a lot of heat and, thanks to media inertia, very little light.

The Canadian media in both Ottawa and Washington did virtually nothing to explain the complexities, consequences and long-term effects on Canadian identity of an agreement that amounted to economic integration with the world's most powerful nation. CBC News, totally silent on the GST issue, also failed, by its own admission, to adequately explain and analyze the free trade question.

That task fell by default to Marjorie Montgomery Bowker, a retired Edmonton judge, who used her own limited resources to publish an independent review and analysis of the Free Trade Agreement.

That job should have been done by the press. It wasn't. The media failed to define the GST issue at all, and failed miserably to deal with free trade in any adequate way.

The issue of press vs. privacy is another thorny issue. Very few Americans were aware until many years after his death that President Franklin D. Roosevelt was crippled by polio and spent much of his time in a wheelchair. Neither foreign nor domestic photographs or newsreels ever showed him in a wheelchair or on crutches. It was only after their deaths that people learned of Harry S. Truman's proclivity for strong

vv

drink and poker, and John F. Kennedy's womanizing. Canadians knew nothing about Prime Minister William Lyon Mackenzie King's spiritualism or that he communicated with his dead mother through his dog Pat.

It probably couldn't happen today. Reporters shrink from such conspiratorial games, but they do agonize over where to draw the line between a public's right to know and a public figure's right to privacy. There is no clear cut line between what is news and what is gossip.

The media were split on the exposé of Gary Hart's extramarital affairs. The paper that broke the story said it did so not because the 1988 American Democratic Party presidential hopeful was having an affair with a woman half his age, but because he lied about it.

The Canadian media had no reservations about splashing Margaret Trudeau's escapades all over the front pages and giving the story full play on radio and TV even though she did not hold public office. The rationale seemed to be that the public had a right to know because her behavior was undoubtedly having an effect on her husband who did hold public office.

In the U.S. interpretation of the moral code on reporting the private lives of public figures is rapidly moving into the realm of sheer sensationalism. Lurid stories that were once the exclusive preserve of the supermarket checkout counters can now be found on the front pages of the *New York Times* and *Washington Post*. What is worse, these stories are often nothing more than the reporting of a tabloid's reporting.

It's difficult for even dictators to keep their skeletons securely locked in the closet anymore. The impoverished Cubans didn't know (and given the country's total press control still don't) that President Fidel Castro and his present wife have five children and, it's reported, 32 houses and 9 700 guards responsible for his safety.

These tidbits were dug up by Komsomolskaya Pravda, one of Russia's publications in the vanguard of that country's new wave journalism. Author A. Novikov writes: "All details concerning the personal life of Fidel Castro and the whole [communist] party elite in Cuba are shrouded in an impenetrable veil of secrecy."

For dictators such secrecy is a matter of survival. Georgie Ann Geyer, author of *Prince, The Untold Story of Fidel Castro,* makes the observation that, "a charismatic leader's power depends on his not being known."

Politicians resent all this scrutiny of their private lives, alleging that it represents nothing less than moral terrorism discouraging good people from entering public service. In many cases they are right. Yet, few responsible journalists would argue for a return to the wink-and-nod attitude toward a leader's behavior. The public still demand high standards from its presidents and prime ministers. It is the media's responsi-

vv

bility to avoid being manipulated into thinking that it is none of the public's business if such standards are violated.

Putting a particular spin on a story is the most common form of manipulation practised by governments of all persuasions. It's done in one form or another in every capital in the world, regardless of a government's political stripe. Getting the right spin on reports means (from the government's point of view) getting the official interpretation on announcements or events into a journalist's reports.

It is an administration's way of getting out its own particular version of the truth under the camouflage of independent and impartial news reports.

How this can be done is limited only by the imagination and enterprise of the "spin doctors." Leaders and their spokesmen may avoid unwanted interpretations by belittling a reporter's questions during news conferences and briefings. It can be a dear-god-spare-me upward rolling of the eyes, or a flippant response like, "the answer to that question should be obvious."

Former Canadian Prime Minister Pierre Trudeau was a past master of the put down. It was a form of intimidation that resulted in fewer questions being asked—questions that needed asking.

Often, when government officials suspect reporters may try to give a story an undesired interpretation, phone calls seeking additional information aren't returned. But when those same officials are determined to inject their own interpretation of statements and comments into the news, they are apt to go to great lengths to track reporters down, and having done so, the reporter who was shunned yesterday is suddenly treated like a long lost buddy.

Members of parliament, congressmen and senators also quickly develop a knack for manipulating the reporter. And there's not much that can be done about it. In the parliamentary system, back benchers have the opportunity to ask the prime minister and cabinet members questions from the floor of the House. Some are intended to embarrass the government, but many are asked for no other purpose than to make the member look good to his constituents back home. If the publicity-seeking member has even a minimal flare for showmanship his query will make at least one of the wire services.

In Washington, most bills die before they get out of the congressional committee stage, but the press they generate makes the initiating congressman or senator look good at home, and assures pressure groups that their elected representative has given their particular concerns his or her best shot.

vv

Non-democratic governments which use state-owned press and broadcasting as mouthpieces for propaganda sometimes ensnare the unsuspecting, inexperienced reporter. The case of former CTV reporter Brian Nelson is a classic example.

Nelson was a member of the media party accompanying then Prime Minister Trudeau on a tour of the Persian Gulf area. At the behest of a special assistant to the Prime Minister, Nelson was asked to read the English language news on state television in Abu Dhabi, capital of the United Arab Emirates. The request for a visiting delegation to provide a journalist to co-host the evening news, he was told, is a traditional diplomatic courtesy in the region.

Given the political volatility of the Middle East such a request, tradition or not, should have raised red warning flags in both the Prime Minister's office and in Nelson's own mind. It didn't. Nelson, who was relatively inexperienced at the time, blithely waded into the newscast. On page 26-B he hit the predictable land mine.

The newscast referred to Israel as a Zionist entity and Prime Minister Shamir as a terrorist. Tiny Abu Dhabi had won a minor triumph, a Western journalist lending credibility in its war of words with Israel.

When word of Nelson's journalistic indiscretion reached the CTV offices in Toronto he and his producer were immediately summoned home. Nelson was fired on the spot, his producer was suspended for six weeks.

The Nelson affair, as it came to be called, became a cause célèbre in press circles. For the most part journalists came to Nelson's defense, including high-profile columnists like Peter Worthington and Douglas Fisher. *Maclean's* suggested CTV had fired Nelson so quickly to neutralize domestic Jewish reaction. Worthington wondered whether the hapless young reporter would have been fired if he had referred to Arafat as a terrorist on Israeli TV. Fisher wrote in the *Toronto Sun* that under the British mandate in Palestine, Shamir had been a terrorist.

The columnists may have had valid points, but they missed entirely the central issue. Correspondents who lend their position and prestige to any cause or point of view being espoused by a foreign government (or anyone) are breaking a fundamental journalistic ethic.

Nelson had been a network correspondent for only two years with no foreign experience when he made his monumental goof. Perhaps under the circumstances CTV could have handled the matter a little less harshly. Fortunately for Nelson, he survived the fiasco with his journalistic ego intact and went on to join the CNN reporting staff in Atlanta.

The Nelson affair gave me a there-but-for-the-grace-of-God feeling. Several years after returning to Canada from a stint as the CBC's

vvv

Moscow-based correspondent, I was told by CBC headquarters that they'd received a request from Soviet television for a Canadian producer-host for a Canada Day special to be produced in the USSR. Would I leave my reporting job for two weeks and take on the project? My first instinct was to say no—give it to an announcer-producer who didn't have a journalistic reputation to worry about. The CBC was insistent. I was the logical choice because I could speak a little Russian, was familiar with the way the Russians did things—and I would have total control over my script. The Soviets were selecting all visual material for the show from CBC and National Film Board libraries.

The first day of videotaping at Moscow's massive Ostankino television studios went without a hitch. The items introduced dealt with such non-controversial subjects as the construction of Toronto's CN Tower, Canadian ballet and an NFB cartoon on ecology. On the second day's taping I was asked to introduce a gentleman who had recently returned from a trip to Canada as a Soviet official, who would recount his experiences. This wasn't part of the deal, especially since the gentleman in question was the editor of *Oktybr*, the Communist Party's unswerving, anti-western ideological monthly. I wasn't concerned about any criticisms of Canada he might have, but I was very much concerned about my appearing to endorse such views and to support Soviet foreign policy.

After solemn assurances that such would not be the case, I agreed to continue taping. Nevertheless, I felt uneasy enough to call Mr. Robert A. Ford, the Canadian ambassador in Moscow, to apprise him of the situation. Since I would be back in Canada by the time the program aired, I asked him if he would kindly monitor the show and let me know if I'd been had. His telex was a tremendous relief. It read:

> Congratulations. Program was well balanced and varied with many items of special interest to Soviet audience. Your remarks were just right. Glad to see your Russian accent is still good. Soviet (editor's) commentary objective although a bit too prolix.
> — R.A.D. Ford.

Before Gorbachev loosened restrictions on the foreign press in the USSR, authorities rewarded, in a variety of ways, correspondents who didn't make waves. An invitation to the space centre, an exclusive interview or access to a "closed" area of the country. The practice is still firmly entrenched in the People's Republic of China.

Democratic states aren't immune from this reward-for-good behavior type of manipulation, but are less blatant about it. Foreign reporters in say London or Washington are already well down on the access-to-information pecking order. Critical reporting can push them even further

vvv

down, maybe even out of sight. Interviews may be abruptly cancelled, questions at news conferences may be ignored, invitations to news briefings or off-the-record sessions don't arrive, and phone calls aren't returned.

This kind of isolation can go on until the powers that be decide the offending reporter has learned his or her lesson. The technique is applied to domestic reporters too, but the damage done to the department or agency doing the isolation is often greater than the punishment inflicted on the reporter. The foreign reporter is much more vulnerable. Less of this kind of vindictiveness can be expected from the newly-emerging democracies of Eastern Europe—at least in the short term, until factions and interest groups become more firmly entrenched and less in need of international publicity.

The Russians recently adopted the Western, or more specifically the American, style of having a full time presidential spokesman. The first man to fill the newly created position was Vitoli Ignatenko. A journalist of some note himself, Ignatenko brought with him an appreciation of reporters' needs. One of his first acts was to establish weekly press briefings. His first promise was openness. "We will not be hiding—we will be open." Only time and events will tell whether his successors follow his example. Russia has no history of a free and independent press. The little freedom there was during czarist times was suffocated and totally suppressed during seven decades of communism. Under Kremlin decree the press became a sycophantic mouthpiece and propaganda arm of the state.

Yet, the hunger for news free of censorship and controls dies hard, and it was the attempted coup of August 1991 that ignited the spark of real journalism in what was then the Soviet Union. A spark that was after all not dead. While the world watched and listened in apprehensive fascination as the country teetered between democracy and resurgent totalitarianism, few were aware that it was a small courageous band of Soviet journalists who worked tirelessly without let up to tell their people and the world what was going on. They told the story from both sides of the barricades factually and dispassionately, even though their very personal and professional survival hung in the balance.

They, and the country's fragile democratic movement, did survive and the leaders of the new Russian journalism won the admiration and respect they richly deserve. Yet their future is far from assured. Few of the newly formed news agencies, like the *Russian Information Agency Ltd.*, expect the current governments to last. The economic collapse and the resultant shortages of food are simply too overpowering for any administration to solve—at least in the short term.

vv

The bleak economic future faced by the government confronts the free press too. At the moment, the independents aren't afraid of being censored or shutdown, but their survival depends on subsidies from the government of the Russian Republic. As this government assumes ever greater direct powers to deal with a desperate life and death situation, it will be tempted to apply Lenin's famous dictum "why should a government which is doing what it believes to be right allow itself to be criticized?" (Especially if that government is paying the critics' bills.)

The germination of an independent press in what was considered sterile Soviet journalistic soil is the real success story of the new Russian Revolution. Yet the philosophy of press as an arm of government dies hard, particularly among journalists who have worked under such a system for their entire careers. While in some instances, like the coup attempt, the work of tough, objective journalists has been nothing short of spectacular, major media institutions are still too uncritical of government and feel a moral obligation to promote the official line. Breaking with this mentality is difficult for any state funded institution.

The big unknown is to what extent the outlawed Communist Party still influences the press. It is generally acknowledged that the cash-rich party which is not supposed to exist continues to secretly fund publications and political movements that are sympathetic to its cause. Whether it again becomes a force to be reckoned with will depend largely on the pace and success of the reforms now being instituted. It cannot be overlooked that hundreds of thousands of government bureaucrats, educators, professional people and industrial managers, who were until quite recently staunch party members, are still in place. They are in a position to exert immense influence on the politics of the Commonwealth of Independent States (CIS).

As mentioned earlier, the tendency to promote government policy is endemic to state media institutions everywhere. In Canada, the CBC was legally mandated to promote national unity until the provision was dropped from the new Broadcasting Act of 1989.

Getting CBC out of the business of promoting this aspect of government policy wasn't universally popular. Harry Boyle, as chairman of the Canadian Radio-television Telecommunications Commission (CRTC) challenged broadcasters, the CBC in particular, to stand up and be counted on national unity. He urged them to go all out to ensure responsible reporting on the issue. He didn't specify who would decide what represented responsible reporting.

The media, state funded or not, should be under no obligation to promote any government policy or program no matter how worthwhile. To do so, is to open the door to intolerable interference and manipulation.

At this writing, only China of all the major international news beats still insists on uncompromisingly tight control of the foreign press, (and its own). News is what the government says it is, not what's actually happening. For foreign broadcast journalists, manipulation is in reality censorship. Television crews are carefully monitored and transmission facilities tightly controlled by the state.

The ultimate weapon of manipulation in closed societies like China is the constant threat of expulsion for any foreign correspondent who insists on reporting on matters the state considers taboo. Political dissent tops the list.

Permission to travel, visit particular institutions or conduct interviews are granted only at the pleasure of the government. Information comes from two main sources, *Xinhau* the official news service and the translations of newspapers—all government controlled. In such situations speaking the language is essential to make contact with ordinary people on the street. It's the only way to find out what's really going on.

Successors to the old Soviet Union, which once taught the Chinese how to handle the foreign press, has made life for its foreign correspondents a lot simpler and easier. There is no longer a need to arrange elaborate ruses to outfox the KGB when correspondents want to meet and talk to ordinary Russians. No more clandestine meetings in parks and under bridges. Gorbachev's glasnost changed all that.

Invitations for foreign correspondents to accompany leaders on trips within the republics are however still hard to come by. Occasionally, they are extended to correspondents from major powers, but are often also inexplicably cancelled. Correspondents from middle powers like Canada are well down on the priority list. Likewise, official leaks when deemed useful to the government are made to influential papers like *The New York Times, The Times* of London *or the Frankfurter Allgemeine.* These leaks may be nothing more than trial balloons. This kind of press manipulation is a first cousin to spin control and is used by every government in the world (also corporations).

In the parlance of government officials, "let's run that idea up the flag pole to see who salutes." A story is planted with a few influential correspondents. If the reaction is negative the planters deny any knowledge of it. If the response is favorable, or even neutral, the issue may be acted upon. Demanding on the record attribution is usually the best way for a correspondent to avoid being used in this way.

Deliberate plants of inaccurate information are the most difficult to deal with. They are used by governments in times of war and peace. Wartime inaccurate information can be particularly effective. When the United Nations set January 15, 1991 as the date for Iraqi withdrawal from

vvv

Kuwait, word went out from the Pentagon to the press that it would likely be several days before air attacks on Iraq would begin. They started in the early morning hours of January 16th, catching Baghdad by surprise. Pentagon officials used the same technique to confuse the Iraqis about the launching time of the ground war.

Manipulation is further achieved by giving exclusive interviews and leaking key information only to favored media outlets, usually major newspapers. The difficulties faced by reporters whose papers or broadcast outlets are not considered to be in the big league is illustrated by the following excerpt from my notes:

> *Moscow*
> Finally got clearance to interview a Soviet cosmonaut/space official. He's Gherman Titov, USSR's second man in space, now on high level planning staff at Star City. Took some doing. First contact two weeks ago somewhat humiliating. Officious fellow on phone wanted to know why Canada interested in space story. "We are not aware you have a space program." he sneered. Guess I did a bit of manipulating myself. "Well no, we don't, but you know we have viewers in the United States. New York for example." (I didn't specify New York State.) Guess that swung it. Interview set for 2 p.m. Wednesday.

Not all governments differentiate between practising spin control and disseminating straight inaccurate information. In pre-Gorbachev days a KGB agent by the name of Victor Louis was assigned to plant erroneous or misleading information among the foreign press corps. Fluent in English, Louis would plant seeds of doubt about sensitive issues in the minds of Western correspondents (especially those newly-arrived in the USSR). Certain prominent people in disfavor with the state, like author Alexander Solzhenitsyn would be skilfully skewered. Damaging rumors about him would inevitably show up in the Western press.

Louis' information wasn't always wrong. When Soviet and Chinese troops clashed on the ice-covered Ussuri River in the winter of 1969, Beijing's embassy in Moscow was the scene of an anti-Chinese demonstration. Louis pulled up in his burnt-orange Porsche to grandly announce that there would be over three thousand demonstrators coming and that about a hundred windows in the embassy would be broken. He was pretty close on both counts. But then why not? He helped organize the entire event.

It's not surprising that police states use people like Louis to throw off foreign reporters trying to ferret out the facts under difficult circumstances. What is surprising is that some western newspapers publish their pronouncements at face value. Victor Louis, known KGB agent, master

vv

of inaccurate information and all round Kremlin fixer was also accredited correspondent of the London *Evening News*.

The advent of Gorbachev's perestroika and glasnost have thankfully curtailed such blatant inaccurate information activities.

It is imperative to point out that for the entire post WW II period precious little in the way of positive news was ever written by Western journalists about the USSR. We all knew what our editors and the public wanted—and it wasn't good news about the Soviets. Reporters are judged by how many stories they get on the air or in print and how many make the lead or the front page. Good stories, especially about communists, don't make the front page. The stories that pleased our editors, and not coincidentally our governments, were about Soviet failures—rotting harvests, laziness, alcoholism, dissidents, anti-semitism and the Gulag. All of us, the Americans in particular, were manipulated by our own selfish interests and perhaps to a lesser extent by social conditioning.

Having said that, it should be made abundantly clear that the old Kremlin leaders didn't make it easy for Western reporters to be objective. There was censorship, harassment, surveillance, paranoic official secrecy and travel restrictions—all conditions that contributed to the overwhelmingly negative and subjective news reporting that came out of the Soviet Union during those years.

Technology and more openness have also poked holes in the old news blackout system. It can no longer be entirely plugged—even by slapping on travel bans. Whether it will accelerate freedom of movement and access to information or bring a clampdown reminiscent of the Stalinist era is as uncertain as the future of Russia itself. No clear cut trend is likely to emerge until the rickety economy is set right, and the fierce political infighting and regional conflicts are settled. What is certain is that, at least for the time being, glasnost has dumped all the old predictable ideological assumptions into the garbage heap. It's a new game in which the rules are still being made up as play progresses. Reaching the present level of press freedom in the former USSR has been a grindingly slow process. It will not be given up lightly.

North Vietnam became expert at manipulating the Western press and influential American public figures during the Vietnam war. It is still doing so. When Hanoi announced in late 1989 that it was pulling its occupation forces out of Cambodia (Kampuchea) journalists from 30 countries converged on the tiny nation to cover the withdrawal. There were waits of up to six hours at the post office in Phnom Penh for use of one of the country's five useable telephone lines. The AP, AFP and *Reuters* news agencies brought in portable satellite uplinks on which other reporters piggy backed stories and pictures. The Vietnamese, not known for their generosity to reporters, proclaimed that in the absence of UN observers and monitoring teams, the verification could be done by journalists. In fact journalists had no way of getting to the areas of rebel action to confirm anything. All tours were arranged by the Hanoi-controlled government and news events were prearranged. All the public saw were pictures of convoys of waving, smiling Vietnamese troops ostensibly going home. As it happened, no one really cared if some of them stayed. Even the Cambodians preferred the Vietnamese to the bloodthirsty Khmer Rouge rebels who threatened to take over again.

When routine manipulation won't work, governments including professed democracies often resort to intimidation, mainly against their own journalists. The true heroes in the continuing international struggle for freedom of the press are not the foreign correspondents, but the thousands of local reporters in the Third World countries and in semi-totalitarian states. These men and women seldom make international headlines.

They are the Palestinian journalist in the occupied Gaza Strip who is jailed because he possesses a fax machine, an essential tool of his trade. The South African publisher who is charged a 15 000 dollar registration fee because the authorities fear the paper will be critical of police and security methods. They are right. The weekly exposes ironclad proof that police death squads have systematically disposed of anti-government trouble makers. Right wing extremists ransack the newspaper offices. It takes the police 20 minutes to get there even though the nearest police station is just around the corner.

The paper is hit with potentially crippling legal costs to defend against libel charges brought by government officials whose own costs are picked up by the taxpayer. All this in a country where the press is supposedly free.

Peru prides itself on having constitutional freedom of the press too. But there's a catch. There is no guarantee of freedom of access, without which press freedom is almost worthless.

Peru's constitutional guarantee of press freedom didn't save Hugo Busteos, a reporter for the Lima based magazine *Caretos*. Busteos was trying to do his job with a deadly brew of drug lords, Maoist guerillas, a corrupt trigger happy military and a weak government. Each faction expects the media to be on its side. Journalists are either for them or against them. There is no middle ground.

The Shining Path guerillas, for example, have no understanding of what a free press is all about. As one Peruvian journalist put it, "They expect us to print or broadcast their manifestos and pamphlets word for word. Of course we can't do that, so they call us enemies of the people and threaten to kill us."

vvv

The military is equally uncompromising. It expects the press to look the other way when atrocities are committed in its unrelenting war against the guerillas. Not to do so is considered treason. It is a war in which suspected guerillas and innocent peasants are gunned down by military death squads.

Hugo Busteos wrote about the peasants' plight, a fact that made him a marked man with the military. It was in these circumstances that Busteos went on his last assignment in November of 1988.

There was a strike in the Arequipa region. Busteos got a report that some peasants had been shot on a dusty rural road. He and a fellow reporter set out on their motorcycle to investigate. As they approached the murder scene they were stopped by the military. They returned a short time later, this time accompanied by the police. The military kicked out both the reporters and the police. Determined to get the facts of the killings, Busteos and his colleagues headed for Bin Los Cabitos, the military's anti-subversive headquarters a few miles away. Here, they were courteously received by the commander and given oral permission to go to the murder site. Busteos asked for written approval. The commander replied with a smile, that would not be necessary. He would simply radio ahead for his men to let two journalists through.

When the two men approached the military road block on their motorcycle a third time, they were met with a hail of automatic fire. "Don't shoot, don't shoot, we're journalists." they shouted. But that's exactly why they were being shot. Busteos died within minutes. His companion was badly wounded, but survived. The camera hanging over his chest stopped the bullets that would have proven fatal.

The military blamed the killings on the Shining Path guerillas. But a number of peasants reported seeing the soldiers change from their uniforms into white T-shirts and jeans before they opened fire from the ditches.

Predictably, the subsequent police investigation was sabotaged. Witnesses who had identified the army captain in charge of the unit involved were arrested, threatened, and in the end, said they had seen nothing. The provincial prosecutor was paralysed. In short, nothing was done. Busteos thus became another in a long list of casualties among Latin American journalists who are trying to do their jobs against tremendous odds.

No more touching epitaph can be given to these courageous reporters than Busteos' own words spoken to his wife days before his death. "I know I am going to die—but I'm going to die for the truth." Hugo Busteos was 38.

vvv

Marites Vitug reports on the environment for the *Manila Chronicle.*
She is risking her career, freedom and life for the rain forest on the
Philippine island of Palawan. The country's largest, the Palawan rain
forest is rapidly falling victim to greed and the chain saw. Its demise also
spells the destruction of the people who live on the island and depend on
the forest for their livelihood and protection from devastating floods and
erosion.

Vitug and *The Chronicle* are determined to save the forest. It's a
daunting assignment. They are taking on one of the Philippines' most
powerful tycoons, one Jose Pepito Alvarez, sole owner of cutting rights
on the island. Alvarez has an ultra cosy relationship with the Speaker of
the Philippine National Assembly, a fellow Palawanian. According to the
Chronicle, Alvarez supplied the Speaker with free vacations and free
helicopter transportation during the last election. He's also been able to
buy off the Church and army.

Vitug ignored death threats and told the story of how endangered
species of trees were being logged, areas where Alvarez had no conces-
sion were being cut, denuded slopes flooded peasant farm lands, and
contrary to law, logs were being exported to Japan. (A country with a
reputation for condoning environmental rape of the world's seas and
forests, if there's a buck in it.)

The story went international when the Hong Kong based *Review*
published an article headlined "The Plunder of Palawan" co-authored by
Vitug and reporter James Clad. It caused a sensation in southeast Asia,
particularly in the Philippines which wasn't enthusiastic about having its
dirty environmental laundry hanging out for all to see.

Philippine officials have a reputation for being fast on the trigger when
it comes to taking libel action. They appreciate the chill effect it has on
journalists. Marites Vitug's case was no exception. She faces libel
charges that if prosecuted successfully could mean years in prison. Libel
in the Philippines is a criminal offense in which malice is presumed. In
other words, the defendant is guilty until proven innocent. Unlike her
co-author, James Clad, who lives abroad, Vitug lives in the Philippines
and is vulnerable. The law suits haven't dampened her spirit, "I can't
leave. It's my country." she says, "If a journalist believes in a story that's
in the public interest, it's worth going to jail for."

Western reporters working abroad also face death or imprisonment as
a consequence of the stories they write. Yet their risks pale in comparison
with what is happening in many countries around the world where the
possibility of being killed, maimed, tortured or imprisoned is a daily part
of a domestic journalist's life. It is the ultimate form of manipulation—the
manipulation of fear.

vv

In the key capitals of the world, the foreign correspondent is resigned to the fact that news conferences and official briefings are basically for the national media of the host country. Foreigners make it a point of not intruding too often. White House news conferences, for example, are attended by large numbers of reporters, both American and foreign. But only a few of the latter get to ask the President a question. Front row seats are reserved for White House "regulars" representing the news organizations with the biggest reach—CBS, NBC, ABC, CNN, *Associated Press, United Press* and *Reuters.* (The latter is British, but is given preferential treatment because of its importance as a world wide news agency.) The rest of the presidential press corps scramble for seats as best they can. And, it's the rare news conference at which a backbencher or foreign correspondent gets to ask a question.

There are some notable exceptions. When President Bush sought and got endorsement from the United Nations Security Council to use force if necessary to get Iraq out of Kuwait, British, French and Soviet reporters were given unprecedented question-access to the president at his next news conference. It was no accident that any one of these countries could have scuttled Bush's U.N. initiative by a veto or that all were in a position to be of considerable military and political help in putting added pressure on Saddam Hussein to vacate Kuwait. Allowing reporters from these countries to ask him questions was Bush's way of saying thanks. As presidential news conferences go, it was a rare happening.

This, however, should not preclude insightful reporting and analysis by a foreign reporter. Knowlton Nash who spent many years as a Washington-based CBC correspondent, feels presidential coverage by Canadians is often better than that of the Americans because their observations are more balanced. Speaking of his own experience, Nash says, "We were not as preoccupied with a narrow particular angle."

American presidents do, from time to time, hold special group interview sessions for resident foreign reporters, but on the whole access is restricted.

This situation is particularly frustrating when the President travels abroad. During the Bush-Gorbachev summit in Malta, White House handlers engaged in what Peter Calami of *Southam News* described as their "customary chauvinism in selecting which journalists could see the leader of the free world in action."

Although the very future of Europe is at stake during such superpower meetings, a reporter from say a Des Moines paper automatically gets a shot on a pool, while correspondents from *The Times* or the *Frankfurter Allgemeine* pick up scraps here and there as best they can. Organizations like *Southam* and CBC aren't even in the running for a pool spot.

vv

In the case of the Malta summit, a planned general briefing for all correspondents, including the Soviets, was cancelled in favor of unofficial background sessions with selected American reporters. This is not an isolated incident. Calami describes this as censorship and manipulation by exclusion.

The 1991 Moscow Summit was even worse. More than 2 000 accredited correspondents were in the Soviet capital to cover the Bush-Gorbachev meeting, but only a select few ever got to actually see the leaders. The common horde was confined to arena-sized press rooms miles from the Kremlin. They didn't even get to see senior aides, let alone Bush and Gorbachev themselves.

Most journalists "covered" the story by hanging around the press room watching CNN TV monitors, interviewing each other and keeping fingers crossed, hoping for at least one briefing by the two press spokesmen.

The arrival of a White House aide with yet another meaningless pool report set off a pushing, shoving, elbowing, feeding frenzy graphically illustrating how far down the news food chain the rank and file reporter really is. Yet correspondents are willing to suffer such indignities and humiliation so they can use prestige sign offs and by-lines to give the illusion that they actually saw and talked to the people that matter.

Like so many major international events of its kind, the Moscow Summit coverage was a big fraud.

It comes as a bit of a surprise that what is commonly called manipulation by consent is so widely practised and accepted as a matter of course in a country like Britain, home of the mother of parliaments. It all revolves around the lobby system. Like so much else in Britain, it operates on the basis of class and snobbery.

A select group of about 150 British reporters are given exclusive access, special perks and inside briefings from which run-of-the-mill reporters are excluded. They are the lobby correspondents.

The important advantage the lobby reporters have is physical proximity to the political news makers. They and they alone among the thousand of British and foreign reporters in the country can mingle with the cabinet and MPs in the Member's Lobby and the forbidden corridors of the Houses of Parliament. (Hence "lobby correspondents.")

There's a price to be paid for such privileged access. Without specific consent, correspondents cannot attribute their stories. Their reports refer to sources "close to the prime minister" or "it is understood that . . . ." Their stories sometimes sound as though they've been mysteriously plucked out of thin air.

Lobby correspondents also must not "see" anything. This means that if an MP or minister falls down drunk in the presence of a reporter, the

vv

reporter hasn't "seen" a thing and wouldn't dream of writing about it. The lobby correspondents in effect see no evil, hear no evil and write no evil.

The practice goes well beyond manipulation to straight news management. What the major papers write, what broadcasters air and what filters down to foreign London-based correspondents has been thoroughly vetted and stage-managed at the source.

This shocking state of affairs can also have a detrimental, if not tragic influence on British correspondents abroad.

On the eve of WW II, the editorials in the *Times* of London and other British papers, no doubt influenced by the Lobby correspondents, assured Britons that Hitler was a man of peace. The line reflected the appeasement policy of the government.

The manipulation was so complete that *The Times* most-celebrated and best-informed correspondent in Berlin found all his insightful dispatches spiked on the editor's desk. Norman Ebbutt was so disillusioned he stopped sending anything of consequence. Frustrated at seeing his stories killed because they didn't square with British foreign policy, Ebbutt turned them over to American reporters. One of the beneficiaries of Ebbutt's work was William Shirer, then a novice reporter in the Nazi maze of intrigue and duplicity. (Shirer would later author the monumental *Rise and Fall of the Third Reich*.) Ebbutt's rationale was that if his paper wouldn't publish his often exclusive and devastating stories, they'd at least see the light of day in North America.

The equanimity with which the British media accepted the near-total news blackout of the Falklands expedition more than 40 years later is a more recent manifestation of the British syndrome of press manipulation by consent.

Nothing surpasses this kind of manipulation so shamelessly as the staged demonstration, whether it's a small local pressure group at home or a politically arranged event involving tens of thousands in some European or Middle Eastern capital. If the TV cameras weren't there, most demonstrations wouldn't take place.

A textbook case was the huge anti-American demonstrations in Tehran during the time American diplomats were being kept prisoners in their embassy by the Ayatollah Khomeini. The crowds were taught to chant in English, and their signs were in English because Farsi wouldn't play well in Peoria. A chant instructor attempted unsuccessfully to go beyond the cliché-worn slogans of "Down with Carter," "Down with America" by introducing a new slogan: "Down with American imperialist cabinet."

vv

An American reporter came to the rescue with something simpler. Within minutes, he had the crowd chanting in unison: "Down with IRS. Down with IRS."

Occasionally the manipulated have the last laugh.

With Friends Like These

> Experience teaches us to be most on our guard to protect liberty
> when governments' purposes are beneficent.
> —Louis Brandeis

"BUSINESSMEN AND TOURISTS BRING DOLLARS, JOURNA-
lists bring trouble. We need dollars. We don't need trouble." With those
words an official of a developing country, perhaps unwittingly, succinctly
summed up the sentiments of most governments towards reporters generally and foreign correspondents in particular. (The latter are harder for
a host country to control.)

Sitting in front of the TV set or scanning the daily newspaper gives the
impression that we truly live in a global village in which technology
mysteriously plucks pictures and words from the sky and deposits them
in our living rooms. Such is, alas, not the case. While words and pictures
do fly around the world with apparent ease, thanks to communications
satellites, the gathering of the news itself is as problematic, if not more
so, than it has ever been.

Journalistic access today is severely restricted or denied in more than
half the countries of the world. Even in countries where a journalist's
passport is routinely stamped, numerous impediments are thrown in the
way. These range all the way from having to pay for official interviews
in democratic Sweden to compulsory registration of visiting journalists
in equally democratic Costa Rica, not to mention the bureaucratic run
around and misleading, self-serving news releases endemic to governments and corporations everywhere in the world.

In the less stable non-democratic states, the reporter faces more menacing obstacles in the form of overt and covert censorship, harassment,
expulsion, imprisonment—even torture and death.

But more is at stake than personal safety and the integrity of the
correspondent. Denial of access, regardless of its form or motivation, is
a denial of freedom of expression, a vital element of the democratic
process and a clear violation of the Universal Declaration of Human
Rights. The declaration's lofty language was, however, of little help for
correspondents who tried to report first-hand Iraq's rape of tiny Kuwait,
or to those journalists who face daily terror from death squads and
murderous drug cartels in South America.

vvv

The danger is often more immediate for reporters working in their home countries, but where local reporters are endangered, foreign journalists have to reckon with similar treatment. They are two sides of the same coin. Of seven journalists kidnapped by the Medellin drug cartel in Colombia in the fall of 1990, six were Colombians, the seventh was a German reporter who was released after being detained for several months.

Yet, the greater the danger, the more vital the presence of the foreign correspondent becomes. Where freedom of the national media has been crushed or severely curtailed, it is the foreign correspondents who become the oppressed people's last hope of truthfully informing the outside world and arousing international public opinion.

This view is echoed by Allain Madoux, head of the Information Department of the International Committee of the Red Cross. "I am convinced," he told a gathering of correspondents, "that by commentaries, by written, recorded or filmed reports that journalists bring back from the actual scenes of conflict, journalists are capable of influencing public opinion, of making people realize not only the horrors of war, but also the reprehensible acts committed by belligerents in defense of international humanitarian law. Whenever journalists witness such violation it is their duty to denounce them."

The United Nations Educational, Scientific and Cultural Organization's commission on world communications, chaired by Sean McBride, underscored that sentiment; "We stress the link between the freedom of the journalist and the freedom of the citizen and reiterate our conviction that the former is an essential feature of a democratic society."

If journalists do in fact play such a crucial role in the promotion and preservation of human freedom and dignity, should they be afforded some kind of special protection, so they can safely go about their job? The chairman of that U.N. Commission thought so. Many of his commission members, however, either had serious doubts or thought any international protection mechanism to be undesirable.

One obvious question immediately arises. How can special protection be arranged or guaranteed? And what price might journalists be asked to pay in return for protection from the state? Journalists themselves have been wrestling with these questions for the past 50 years. They have tried through their professional organizations and through international bodies to find ways to mitigate the dangers and opposition they encounter in the performance of their duties. The issue has also resulted in a wide-ranging debate outside the profession. Suggestions have been made that reporters carry special banners in battle zones (like the Red Cross) or wear distinctive badges (tried during WW I).

vv

All efforts by the UNESCO commission to come up with a convention to protect journalists on dangerous missions have foundered at the draft stage. The *Council of Europe's* attempts concerning foreign correspondents have been equally unsuccessful. The Additional Protocol to the Geneva Conventions of August 1949 has come the closest to some form of official safety guarantee for correspondents. It stipulates that journalists on dangerous professional combat assignments are to be considered as civilians and protected as such. There are exceptions. A correspondent who attaches him or herself to a military unit cannot expect to be immune from enemy attack. Likewise, correspondents who take an active part in hostilities, as some did in the Korean war and Vietnam, cannot be assured of protection as civilians. Armed forces retain the right to apprehend reporters who are found in a military zone—to ensure personal safety if nothing else.

The Geneva Conventions are somewhat vague on the rights of the journalists involved in civil wars. Detainees are supposed to be treated humanely. But during internal armed conflicts such as in Lebanon, there's not much anyone can do about unjustified or prolonged detention. In civil wars, governments and insurgents make their own rules without regard for international conventions.

International law explicitly prohibits the taking of hostages. But for people like Terry Anderson of *Associated Press*, such laws were of little comfort.

There are no guarantees for journalists caught in a war zone. But it is the International Committee of the Red Cross which has been most helpful in providing journalists with the basic elemental protection: finding the whereabouts of those who have disappeared, notifying families and employers, making every attempt at humane treatment for those imprisoned and conducting behind the scenes negotiations for release.

Perhaps most important of all in obtaining a journalist's release is the pressure of public opinion. Here, the media themselves must become their own protector. Allain Madoux of the ICRC puts it this way:

> *I am convinced that public opinion conditioned by the media, is an excellent means of bringing pressure on belligerents and is capable of favorably modifying the attitude of combatants to victims protected by humanitarian law.*
>
> *In a world where the rules of the Geneva Conventions are often ignored, when the international community too often shows its powerlessness in the face of repeated violations of humanitarian rules, no matter how universally accepted they may be, the judgment of the public opinion is finally the most effective sanction—or from another point of view the least ineffectual.*

vv

The most contentious aspect of the continuing debate on the safety of journalists is the proposal to issue state identity cards to journalists. The intention being that these would facilitate access and assure protection. This approach, has been almost universally rejected by rank and file reporters who see it as state control in the form of licensing leading to self-censorship.

Licensing journalists is nothing new. It has been a standard practice in non and semi-democratic states for some time. The alarming thing is that the practice is spreading, especially in Latin America, Africa and Asia. In countries where journalists require a license to work, they invariably keep their jobs at the pleasure of the state. What is given can also be taken away—and often is.

Recently, a group of journalists in Zimbabwe exposed an automobile black market ring involving a number of cabinet ministers in Robert Mugabe's government. The ministers, who had purchasing priority, allegedly bought cars directly from the plant, then sold them at inflated prices to car-hungry customers whose names were on a long waiting list.

The exposé had barely begun before government pressure forced state-employed reporters to call it off. The journalists who had the temerity to do what journalists are supposed to do, investigate, had their permits lifted. The lucky ones were transferred to the government's information department. Others were fired. Such a distinct possibility of losing one's job certainly discourages investigative journalism.

The majority of members on the UNESCO commission on the international media came to the same conclusion with the observation that, "experience shows that the granting of professional licences and all complicated accreditation procedures tend to foster government intervention in the national and international flow of news."

Journalists do not want special privileges or favors. Accepting special treatment can lead to government regulation and official monitoring of reporters' professional conduct. They are especially fearful that any kind of licensing system would allow governments or their agencies to decide who can and who cannot practise journalism. As matters stand now, a person is a journalist simply by virtue of his or her employment. (In some countries membership in a union or professional association is required.) Journalists fear that any licensing scheme could mean only those journalists with the government's "good housekeeping" seal of approval would (a) be protected and (b) be allowed to work. (Journalists expect reasonable access as a matter of course and the same physical protection afforded any citizen.)

The journalists' fears are not unfounded. The UNESCO commission's original draft linked protection of journalists with special identification

vv

cards and a universal code of conduct. Both imply that in return for protection, journalists would come under at least a degree of government control, by being obliged to accept certain political and diplomatic obligations and be required to abide by what the drafters of the document decreed to be journalistic morality and social awareness. The draft and subsequent revisions were summarily rejected by democratic governments, including Canada, by the Western journalistic fraternity, and by members of the commission itself.

The right for anyone to be a journalist does not imply that there should not be professional standards and laws under which reporters work. Journalists, like everyone else, are subject to laws of libel, slander and other restrictions placed upon them by law. Nor can their rights to access be unconditional. Sovereign states reserve the right to impose restrictions in such areas as the military and diplomacy.

In countries where constitutions guarantee freedom of speech, and a free press, and where governments abide by such constitutions, the persevering reporter is usually able to his or her job. The dilemma arises when that reporter is assigned to a country where the law is ignored or the law itself prohibits or inhibits the free flow of information in contravention of the Universal Declaration of Human Rights. The snag here lies in the interpretation of these documents. The ICRC, for instance, stipulates that freedom of expression carries with it special duties and responsibilities which translate into certain restrictions. These include "the protection of national security, of public order and of public health and morals." These caveats to the free flow of news are open to whatever interpretation a state chooses. All too often, there is a tendency in all countries to keep the lid on certain information on the specious grounds of that favorite catchall called "national security." Journalists naturally recognize the official secrecy rule for what it often is—an attempt to cover up corruption, inefficiency or some other misdeed, and go ahead with the story in defiance of government authority. That is when they run afoul of either their own government, their host government or both. In such cases it is usually left up to the courts to decide whether some kind of security breach has occurred.

The American Convention on Human Rights (signed in 1969) stipulates that the right of freedom of expression is not subject to prior censorship but to subsequent imposition of liability as established by law. The convention lays down a number of ground rules with which ethical journalists should have no trouble. Offenses punishable by law include ". . . advocacy of national, racial or religious hatred that constitute incitements to lawless violence or any other similar illegal action against

 vv

any person or groups of persons on any grounds including those of race, color, religion, language or national origin."

Efforts to establish a universal code of professional ethics for journalists has been as contentious as the licensing issue. National or regional codes already exist in more than 60 countries. Canada has no national code. But during the past 20 years press councils have been set up in all provinces except Saskatchewan. Made up of publishers, journalists and members of the general public, they hear and adjudicate complaints about the print media's conduct and performance. Broadcast companies, both private and public, also have bureaus to investigate complaints.

Since 1982 the Canadian Charter of Rights has greatly expanded media rights, and at the same time "the public's right to know." This greater access underlines the need for a national code of ethics and better mechanisms for handling public complaints. These codes are usually drawn up and adopted by the journalists' own professional organizations. In too many instances though, they are unfortunately imposed either by law or government edict. These state-imposed codes invariably include such universally accepted principles as objectivity, fairness, balance, freedom of information and access, truthfulness, protection of courses and right of privacy. Often, however, wording is vague and open to wide-ranging interpretation. In 1971, a code of professional ethics was prepared for Arab journalists within the Arab League. It contains all the high-minded principles of freedom of information and fundamental human rights generally associated with a free and responsible press. Yet nowhere is the press more servile and propagandistic than in many of these very same Arab states.

A number of professional codes, particularly those in developing countries, include special provisions for the promotion and protection of cultural, social and ethnic values. These may be laudable goals but hardly the responsibility of journalists.

The lobbying efforts for some kind of international licensing system and code of ethics comes primarily from the world's less developed nations. As their political clout grows within such international organizations as UNESCO, concern about their image abroad, particularly in the West, also increases. The most common complaint is that Western coverage is limited, biased, unbalanced and distorted. Furthermore, these countries see foreign news coverage of their countries as being sensational and crisis oriented.

At least some of their allegations are borne out by media studies on the subject. Others are not. In 1981, the American team on a UNESCO-sponsored study found that the volume of news from less developed countries carried by *Associated Press* and *United Press International*

vv

(both U.S. news services) was actually greater than from developed countries.*

This finding, however, does not necessarily negate charges from Third World media critics. What appears on the AP and UPI wired (both are also basic Canadian foreign news sources) is one thing, what editors select to run in their newspapers and on news broadcasts is quite another. Given the cultural ties with Europe, Canadian and American editors tend to consider stories from that area more important than news from developing countries.

The survey data also confirmed the claim that Western news agencies focus on crisis and conflict in the Third World. This may be because there is more conflict and crisis in these countries. Examples abound—the Vietnam war, the Iranian hostage crisis, revolution in the Philippines, the Tiananmen Square massacre in China, civil war in Central America and the Iraqi invasion of Kuwait. That having been said, it is important to point out that news coverage of developed countries also concentrates on crime, military activity and the bizarre. Cultural, scientific and medical achievements are given secondary treatment as they are everywhere.

Allegations from developing countries that they usually come off looking like second class citizens are not entirely groundless either. Consider the coverage of two major international news stories by the *International Herald Tribune* in one of its February 1990 editions. Seven of its eight columns were devoted to the Palestinian uprising. The headline read; *Israeli Soldier Shot to Death. Palestinian Toll Rises to 96.* The eighth column reported that 5 000 Kurds had died in an Iraqi gas attack. A ferry sinking in the English Channel gets considerably more attention in the Western press than a similar tragedy somewhere in Asia, even though the death toll in the latter may be much higher.

Nothing much will change in the way the Western media cover the Third World as long as they reflect and emulate the ambivalent attitudes of their governments. When Pierre Trudeau, former Prime Minister of Canada, was asked to comment on the war in Biafra his typically sarcastic reply was, "where's Biafra?" He knew very well where Biafra was but his rhetorical question really conveyed the message that he didn't give a damn about the civil war then raging in Nigeria and most definitely not the interests of Biafrans.

Neither Canada nor most of the rest of the world cared much about the invasion of East Timor by Indonesian forces in 1975 either. Where is East Timor, and why should anyone care about it? It's the eastern half of a

---

* In 1992 Saudi Arabian investors bought UPI. They pledged to retain the agency's international character, but will emphasize news from the Third World and on the environment.

vvv

large island north of Australia, and since Indonesia invaded the former
Portuguese colony thousands of people have been killed. The fighting
goes on, but it continues to be a non-story in the West. Unlike the Iraqi
invasion of Kuwait, according to one senior CBC producer, the public
can't "connect" with East Timor. That's hardly surprising because they
haven't heard about it and aren't likely to because for the media East
Timor, like hundreds of other remote places in the world is a "non-
agenda" location. Furthermore, Canada like most other Western countries tilts heavily in favor of Indonesia because we are loath to jeopardize
our financial investments in that country.

The forceful annexation of East Timor by Indonesia did briefly make
headlines when five correspondents were killed covering it. Two Australian TV news teams, made up of Greg Shackelton, Gary Cunningham,
Tony Stewart, Malcolm Rennie and Brian Peters, all died in an unused
house overlooking the Indonesian landing zone. The word Australia and
an Australian flag were emblazoned on one side. Their bodies were found
burned beyond recognition hours after the launch of an early morning
artillery, mortar and tank attack.

No one knows how they died. One story is that Indonesian troops fired
into the building killing everyone inside; another that the reporters were
gunned down as they fled the building; yet another that they were lined
up and executed.

The most likely scenario is that the five died in the heat of battle. After
realizing that the building had housed journalists, not East Timorese
soldiers, the Indonesians tried to destroy the evidence by burning the
bodies and the television equipment.

The correspondents' courage cannot be questioned. Their judgment
can. The tragic irony is that the Australian crews were killed by the very
forces being given tacit support by their own government in Canberra.

Efforts by human rights groups to focus attention on what's going on
in obscure places like East Timor have been to no avail. Noble words like
"freedom" and "independence" may have meaning when applied to the
newly emerging democracies of eastern Europe, or even to the Middle
East when self-interest is at stake, but they mysteriously lose their
relevance for people in those out of the way corners of the world not on
our government's nor the media's agenda.

The Western media practice a double standard in their coverage of
international events in other ways too. Canadian journalist Peter Trueman, in his book *Smoke & Mirrors*, comments on what has become
known as the Afghanistan principle. He says of Canadian journalists,
"We tend to be absolutely fearless about reporting unsavory truths about
Zimbabwe, or even Chicago. Much of the time we don't maintain the

vvv

same standard at home." An American colleague of mine describes the Afghanistan principle in more earthy terms—"the closer you get to home the harder they (editors) squeeze your balls."

That was certainly the philosophy at CBC. George Davidson, a former CBC president, told Canadian Press during the 1970 FLQ crisis in Quebec that it was one thing to tell Canadians about such insurgencies in foreign countries but quite another when they are happening in our own backyard.

It is precisely this kind of double standard and lack of positive news that has prompted the Third World countries to be so vociferous in their demands for a universal licensing system and code of ethics for foreign correspondents. It's unlikely to happen. The problem lies not so much in the volume of news generated in developing nations, as in basic questions of news values and judgments of media editors. Cultural affinities aside, radically different views of what constitutes news exist among all countries—not just between the haves and have-nots, even though it is most apparent in the latter case.

This is essentially the conclusion reached by UNESCO's study of the international media. It speaks of the incompatibility between two essentially distinct conceptions of journalism rather than an incompatibility between the ethical proposals themselves. The commission felt, however, that the pursuit of an international code of journalistic ethics should not be abandoned.

Ellie Abel, a veteran American journalist and UNESCO commission member disagrees. In a minority comment, Abel summed up his feelings on the matter this way:

> *A planetary code for journalists of all nations is neither attainable nor desirable in present circumstances. There are indeed two essentially distinct conceptions of journalism in the world today. Where the press is the arm of the state, there can be no room for the exercise of independent professional judgment by journalists. A code of ethics that would be compatible with such a system of political control must necessarily be rejected by journalists who see their role as independent of the state and, indeed, as decently skeptical of government authority.*

Like individuals, societies have difficulty seeing themselves as others see them. Scottish poet Robert Burns put it most eloquently when he wrote:

> *Oh wad some power the giftie gie us*
> *To see oursels as ithers see us!*

vvv

This inability to see within ourselves what others perceive most clearly is just as applicable among Western societies as it is vis-à-vis the have and have not countries.

Nothing evokes this defensive streak as quickly as the exchange of TV documentaries among nations. Less frequent today than they were in the early days of television, these exchanges are designed to promote international understanding. They say in effect, "I'll tell you exactly what I think of you, and you tell me what you really think of me." Societies, like individuals, seldom like what they hear.

Intertel was one of the most ambitious international exchanges of this kind ever attempted. It involved the four major English-speaking countries of the world—the United States, Canada, Britain and Australia. All these countries share, besides a common language, the same basic social and cultural values. It was the kind of mix in which well-intentioned producers could examine a particular issue and make social, political and cultural judgments on another member's country. At least that was the idea.

American Educational TV network and Westinghouse Broadcasting Company (the U.S. partners) thought the Canadian Broadcasting Corporation's documentaries on American issues failed to comprehend what documentary analyst A. William Bluem called, "the circumstances which lead American life pattern and social policies." In short, they didn't like what the Canadian producers had to say about the United States, not the way they said it. The American TV outlets declined to run several programs.

Bluem says two Canadian documentaries in particular irked the Americans—both produced by Douglas Leiterman. One entitled *One More River* dealt with the 1960s American civil rights struggle. American broadcast executives rejected it outright for "heavy handedness and indiscriminate taste." They expressed resentment that Leiterman had ventured into a crucial area of public policy alleging a less than objective viewpoint which was highly colored by "art-for-art's sake."

Another CBC production, *Cuba Si* (the "Yanqui non" was implied) got a similarly cold reception from the Americans. As the title suggests, the program did not support American policy toward Castro's Cuba. At first the program was "delayed for revisions," then it was quietly dropped from the schedule.

Looking at another country from a distance can be illuminating, like looking from the dark into the light. If, however, the foreign producer/reporter fails to pick up on the delicate subtleties and peculiarities of national characteristics and circumstances, the result may resemble caricature more than reality.

vvv

This happened when an American crew decided to take a look at socioeconomic change in Britain. The location chosen to shoot *Post Script to Empire* was the Isle of Dogs, which is not exactly representative of British society. An elderly ultra-conservative couple railing against the encroachment of labor unions in their community represented the old guard. A young couple who had sought a brighter future in a new modern industrial community nearby represented the new wave. This particular American view of the British no doubt annoyed, perhaps even amused, but didn't do much to enlighten the British on their changing society. As for viewers on the other side of the Atlantic, the program entrenched an already stereotyped view of a class-ridden British society.

A British documentary on Canada-U.S. relations, *Living with a Giant,* revived the perennial debate about what makes Canadians different from Americans. It succeeded in focusing on the central question of whether the "mouse" sharing a bed with the "elephant" can survive. The documentary dealt competently with such basic issues as American economic dominance and the flood of American television programs and publications pouring across the border. It did not articulate why Canadians feel Canadian and not American, primarily because the Canadians who appeared on the program themselves failed to do so.

My own reports and programs on foreign issues have, at times, also met with something less than an enthusiastic response from those directly involved.

In 1971, I was the reporter on a CBC television documentary which examined the civil strife in Northern Ireland. The program, *The Sleepy Grass,** provoked strong reaction from Ulster Protestants in Canada, who accused producer Martyn Burke and me of getting it all wrong. The BBC's initial interest in airing the Canadian viewpoint of the trouble faded quickly after the first screening. The program deplored IRA tactics, but allowed the IRA to state their position. Apparently the BBC thought we got it all wrong too. The basic point of disagreement seemed to be over whether the bloodshed and violence has its base in the way people worship—Protestant vs. Catholic—or in Ulster's socioeconomic and political structure which for historical reasons relegates Catholics to second-class citizenship. My notes during the assignment leave no doubt on my particular outside viewpoint. It hasn't changed.

---

* Irish legend has it that every so many years a magical mist falls on
  Ireland's plants and grass, producing a narcotic effect resulting in strange
  behavior by the populace.

vv

August 10/71

I came here convinced like so many reporters, that religion was at the heart of all the troubles. The Protestants hate the pope-loving Catholics and Catholics despise the Protestant infidels. I haven't met anyone Catholic or Protestant who gives a damn about how anyone worships. The rabid Ian Paisley and his Protestant extremist followers may be an exception but I suspect even Paisley uses the religious issue as a prop for his hate crusade.

Was surprised to find that all Irish revolutionaries weren't Catholic. As far back as the late 18th century Protestant Wolfe Tone formed the United Irish Society which tried to unite Protestants and Catholics in a bid to overthrow English rule. In 1916, Ulster Protestant and British career diplomat Sir Roger Casement was hanged for aiding the Irish rebellion against Britain.

Both men are now part of the Catholic rebels' pantheon of revolutionary heroes. On a more personal level, the driver who took me to an IRA hideout last Monday told me he was a Protestant married to a Catholic girl.

Tend to agree with the archbishop when he says that labels, Protestant and Catholic, simply delineate the haves and have-nots. The Protestants, mainly descended from English and Scottish settlers brought in and established in positions of power by England's Oliver Cromwell are today's haves. The descendants of the defeated indigenous Irish (Catholics) are the have-nots. Catholics, frustrated, consider themselves second class citizens and most want union with Irish Republic to the south. Protestants who tend to consider themselves culturally superior to Catholics would be a minority in a united Ireland. They're determined to stay part of Britain—not so much because they're such loyal subjects of Her Majesty, but the Union Jack provides the shield behind which they can hold onto their privileged position.

Emotions run high on both sides resulting in bloodshed and mayhem all around. Over religion though? Religion may affect some individual viewpoints, but in my book the fight revolves around social and economic issues at the grass roots and in a larger sense around the issue of Catholic nationalism (union with the South) and Protestant unionism (staying part of Britain).

The following story, probably apocryphal, was making the rounds among reporters in Ulster when I was there. A Canadian reporter is sitting alone in a Catholic pub. One of the locals comes over and asks:

"Where you from?"

"I'm a Canadian reporter."

"You a Catholic or Protestant?"

Not wishing to start trouble the reporter replies, "I'm an agnostic."

vvv

The local rolls this over in his mind for few seconds then says, "Now would that be a Catholic agnostic or a Protestant agnostic?"

Trying to plumb the depths of the Irish soul can be a daunting experience. But the problem with *The Sleepy Grass* pointed up the inherent difficulty with any international exchange of documentaries, and all foreign reporting. The Irish Protestants who saw the program resented it. The BBC rejected it. The Americans turned thumbs down on the CBC's interpretation of racial integration on *One More River*. The British didn't appreciate being caricatured by the Americans in *Postscript to Empire* and many Canadians thought the British view of our relationship with the United States in *Living with a Giant* was wide of the mark.

In spite of all the shortcomings of these programs and foreign reporting in general, any move toward national or international legislation to make foreign reporting fit accepted perceptions must be vigorously opposed. Often these outside viewpoints are resented precisely because they shine light on a dark corner which those closest to it cannot or prefer not to see. The foreign observer may, at times, miss some of the subtleties and nuances of his subject, but the dictum that "they see farther looking out of the dark into the light than those in the light looking upon the light" applies in no small measure to international journalism.

Different Strokes

Why should freedom of speech and freedom of the press be allowed? Why should a government which is doing what it believes to be right allow itself to be criticized? It would not allow opposition by lethal weapons. Ideas are much more fatal things than guns. Why be allowed to buy a printing press and disseminate pernicious opinions calculated to embarrass the government.
—Vladimir Lenin

"WHY CAN'T THEY BE MORE LIKE US?" IS A THEME THAT runs through the mind of every reporter who is sent abroad. Complaints about official restrictions in Canada pale in comparison to the obstacle courses the correspondent must manoeuvre in foreign lands.

It's taken for granted that hard core communist states like the People's Republic of China, North Korea, Vietnam and Cuba will be less than hospitable. So will the one-party African states that embrace Lenin's uncompromising stand against a free press.

What comes as a rude jolt is the obsequious nature of the media in many Western democracies. In Britain, France and Germany, reporters have a disturbing habit of accepting government announcements and handouts at face value with little in the way of critical analysis or questioning.

In Britain papers that run riot with rumors and tittle-tattle fall strangely silent when those same rumors turn out to be true. The British press also has a way of not letting facts get in the way of a good story.

During the 1961 trial in Moscow of American U-2 spy plane pilot Francis Gary Powers, a British reporter said he saw Powers' wife, Barbara, wipe away tears when the verdict was read. An American reporter present protested, "You can't write that, I was there and she didn't cry." The British reporter thought for a moment, then replied, "Well, if she didn't, she should have."

Incidents like that prompted a Canadian reporter friend of mine to label the British press "the whores of Fleet Street." Most journalists would be a bit more charitable by suggesting that the British are better writers (which they are) and North Americans are better reporters (which they are).

A major complaint of reporters working abroad, especially the Americans, is lack of access. But what American reporters fail to realize is that foreign reporters working in the United States face the same problem.

RAESIDE
Victoria Times-Colonist

vvv

Foreigners are of course free to report on what they see and learn in the United States, but accessing the right people and events to put flesh and bone on a story is usually difficult and sometimes impossible.

Of all the democracies, Israel imposes the severest restrictions on both its own media and the foreign press. The New York-based *Committee to Protect Journalists* includes Israel among the 16 states it singles out for "concern." The Committee's 1990 report found that media restrictions in Israel are wide ranging throughout the country, with extremely severe limitations applied in the occupied territories.

Palestinian journalists are routinely detained on the assumption that they are using their profession as a cover for intifada activities. Articles in Hebraic reprinted in Arabic language newspapers are often removed by censors. Censorship also applies to the Hebrew press, but is less rigidly applied.

Reporting on such controversial subjects as Russian-Jewish immigration is restricted, and reporters trying to do stories on Jewish settlements in the occupied lands face abuse from the settlers as well as the possibility of police detention.

In 1990, according to the CPJ report, nine Arab journalists were detained for up to 11 months; one Arab paper was shut down; one Israeli state TV editor was fired for allegedly writing pro-Arab articles and two Israeli reporters were attacked by settlers at the Ariel Jewish settlement in the occupied territories.

Foreign correspondents are usually given greater freedom to report than Israeli reporters, but they too must abide by the rules of censorship and regulated access. Nor is physical violence against foreign reporters unheard of. In 1990, Canadian photographer Karen Lagerquist working for *Agence France Presse* was severely beaten by a police officer in East Jerusalem. The police confiscated her film and threatened her with expulsion from the country.

Other states that pose either a threat to journalists' personal safety or their freedom to report, or both, are Cuba, Guatemala, Myanmar (Burma), Romania, Yugoslavia, Saudi Arabia, India, Iraq, Kenya, Lebanon, Liberia, Sudan, most African countries, Colombia and China. Key areas for the international journalist which are generally considered hardship posts merit particular attention.

Russia and Ukraine

The first shock for the correspondent taking up a posting in Moscow is the depressingly run-down condition of this ancient capital city. Old buildings, grand edifices during the days of the czars are crumbling. Their facades, formerly painted in shades of Easter egg pastels, are faded and peeling. Large chunks of stucco are breaking off walls which are rarely

vv

repaired. New structures show signs of deterioration even before they are occupied.

Streets are clogged with traffic, mainly trucks spewing clouds of black exhaust into an atmosphere already polluted by heavy industrial and coal-fired power plants located inside the city. Potholes dot a disintegrating road system like some carefully laid out minefield.

Foreigners are advised not to rent the top floors of an apartment building because the roof invariably leaks and antiquated elevators are chronically stuck. Flats in specially designated compounds for foreigners are cramped two-bedroom units which each occupant renovates to Western standards. Furniture, carpets, drapes and appliances are imported, usually from one of the Scandinavian countries because the waiting list for these items in the Republics can be longer than the average correspondent's posting. In any event, the quality of Russian-made goods in unacceptable to most foreigners.

By Moscow standards, apartments reserved for foreigners are roomy and luxurious. In 1920, Lenin decreed that the housing norms for adequate living space would be nine square metres—or the equivalent of a ten-by-ten foot room, per person. Seventy years later, many Russians in urban centres have yet to reach that minimum.

As the fledgling capitalist economy finds its wings, a wider variety of merchandise is filtering into once empty shops along Moscow's showplace Kalinin Prospekt and St. Petersburg's famous Nevsky. But it hasn't much helped the ordinary Russian, who is still in the cold because prices for most goods are well beyond reach.

There's an added frustration. Many of Russia's new entrepreneurs-cum-hustlers demand hard currency—preferably American dollars. Offering rubles is tantamount to an insult. Under communism people had money in their pockets but nothing to buy. Now there's something to buy, but they have no money.

The chaotic economy of skyrocketing prices and uncertain supply also makes life difficult for the foreign resident trying to maintain a decent diet and work within a reasonable budget. For the foreigner, the days when a few packs of Marlboros would pay for a cab fare or buy a couple of theatre tickets are gone. American cigarettes are plentiful and cheaper than in Canada. A good bottle of scotch, though, still works wonders when a leaky faucet needs fixing or a windowpane has to be replaced.

A lack of incentives permeates the entire society, resulting in shoddy workmanship all along the line from shoes to ships. It is precisely this malaise that Robert Ford, former Canadian ambassador to the Soviet Union, blames for the astounding number of transportation and industrial

vvv

accidents which plague the country, including the calamitous meltdown at the Chernobyl nuclear power station.

A full-time driver is a practical necessity for correspondents in Moscow. The mails are undependable and not widely used within the cities. There are no courier services, so the newsroom driver makes pickups, pays the bills and delivers the inter-city mail. He argues down the customs agents who aren't above holding up a shipment until a few rubles pass under the table. It's the driver who takes the kids to school in the morning and picks them up at four. He arranges for car repairs and servicing and scours the city for some hard to get item like a kitchen mop. He's the all-round fixer who knows all the phone numbers that matter in a country that still doesn't have phone books. The Russian government hopes all these shortcomings will be rectified under a market-driven economy.

Motorists' driving habits in Moscow border on the suicidal. Night driving is particularly hazardous because only parking lights are allowed, an apparent hangover from the WW II blackout years. A thoughtless foreigner driving with his dims on will get a rapid flashing of headlights, much as our motorists do when hit with the full glare of brights. Add the vagaries of Russian driving regulations and you've got motoring madness unlike anything in the world, with the possible exceptions of Italy and the Middle East.

Logistical problems involved in day-to-day life are so complex that they easily chew up a correspondent's entire working day, leaving little or no time for serious journalism which is, after all, the reporter's purpose in being there in the first place.

The solution lies in delegating as many time-consuming administrative and housekeeping chores as possible to the driver, secretary and maid. Yes, a maid. They're easily affordable and are worth their weight in gold rubles. The maid stands in the ubiquitous shopping lines, baby-sits, serves at dinners and cocktail parties. The maid, the driver and secretary were formerly all required to report their employer's activities to the security police. It was a minor irritant that went with the territory and is now thankfully a thing of the past.

Education can be a headache for correspondents with school-aged children. Nationals whose countries can't afford to set up private schools send their grade school children to the Anglo-American School essentially operated by the Americans and British. The curriculum is heavily U.S. orientated. Students come from 25 to 30 different countries, which gives the school the appearance and atmosphere of a United Nations in miniature. Some correspondents prefer to enrol their children in the nearest Russian public school, where of course all instruction is in

vv

Russian. High school students either continue their education in their home countries, or enrol in private schools in Western Europe.

While Moscow is considered a hardship post for correspondents, it is not without benefits. The capital is ringed with numerous green belts and is surrounded by woods that make hikes, picnicking or cross-country skiing a delight. The ballet, opera and theatre are first class and easily affordable. The Russian people, particularly in the smaller cities and in the countryside, are warm and hospitable. Travel arrangements can be a problem, but once overcome the adventure of a lifetime awaits the traveller in the great Russian outback of Siberia—in Russian it is *Sibir*, the sleeping giant.

The reinvented Soviet Union will continue to be one of the most fascinating of all global beats. The former republics, not least of all the giant Russian Federation itself, are embarked on a course of nation building that is exhilarating and at the same time frightening. A hundred ethnic nationalities are openly debating their futures. All too frequently words give way to violence. For the correspondent it means a front row seat for history in the making.

To report intelligently on events in this fallen superpower it is crucial to understand its past. It isn't enough to follow the daily comings and goings of the Gorbachevs, Yeltsins, Kravchuks and their successors. Western correspondents may be absorbed with the degree of democratization being carried out by this or that leader but like the undercurrent of a large river, the force and direction of the flow will be largely determined by the people themselves.

The thirst for Western-style institutions propelled by Western political and economic principles among the former Soviet citizens is overestimated in the West. Food and housing are the immediate concerns of the ordinary Russian, yet the people possess a spirituality and sense of national destiny that is quite foreign to the rest of the world. It is almost medieval in nature.

As they have so often in their turbulent history, Russians are once again turning to the church for guidance, comfort and perhaps most important of all a sense of destiny. Recent polls suggest that the Russian Orthodox Church is the most trusted institution in the country today. Most telling of all is the fact that after a millennium and a half the liturgy of the Church that appeals so profoundly to the senses as well as the spirit has changed very little.

Nor has the Russian messiah complex changed. In old Russia the people looked to the church for their sense of community and that community feeling, called *sobornost* dictated strong but benevolent leadership which has paradoxically eluded the people throughout their

vv

history. For all that, Russians have traditionally looked to a strongman to bring order out of chaos, as Stalin did. Many Russians are more deeply suspicious of Western influence on their society than they are of dictatorial tendencies within their leadership. They cast a jaundiced eye on the new business entrepreneur, often a former communist bureaucrat who accumulated capital at the public trough during the party's heyday. They see a market economy pushing chronic food shortages to the brink of starvation and with it the risk of civil disorder.

Many reporters overlooked the fact that the coup of August 1991 was crushed by only several thousand members of the Moscow intelligentsia. Two hundred and eighty million others looked on impassively from the sidelines.

These same tens of millions complain about the deplorable living conditions they endure and clamor for somebody in authority—anybody—to "fix the system," as one Russian journalist put it. When they are told that under glasnost and perestroika it is they who are ultimately responsible for creating a more abundant and comfortable life, they say: "Me? Why we have never had to look after our own welfare. It's always been done for us. There must be somebody in authority who can do something to give us more food, housing and better consumer goods."

Telling the people that they are part of both the problem and the solution doesn't go down well on the street. Gorbachev wasn't able to generate much personal participation. It will be an uphill battle for his successors too.

Work for the correspondent in Moscow is stimulating and exciting, particularly at this stage in Russian history. This nation is again at a historical crossroads. Whichever path it chooses will have an impact not only on its own people in its disintegrating republics, but on the world as a whole.

The country is openly debating its future. Unfortunately words are giving way with disturbing frequency to violence. For the correspondent, it means a front row seat for history in the making.

China

It's no coincidence that China handles foreign correspondents in much the same manner as the Russians once did because Moscow designed the system for them. Specific areas are designated for foreign residents and offices by a state agency in charge of outsiders. The same agency provides state-approved staff. Police surveillance and an inborn xenophobia nourished by centuries of external intrusion ensures limited contact between the foreign reporter and the people. Travel outside Beijing and all interviews are carefully controlled.

vvv

Totalitarian systems find fertile ground in societies that have no deep-rooted tradition of free journalism. The ability of foreign reporters to do their job is determined in direct ratio to the actual freedoms enjoyed by the local press. China is no exception.

China has no tradition in journalism. The profession was brought into the country as a transplant by the British some hundred years ago, first to Hong Kong ,then later to treaty ports like Shanghai. Chinese authorities, then as now, regard journalism as a profession of questionable respectability. Foreign reporting from inside China was and is seen as an activity akin to espionage.

In a country where policy is traditionally the prerogative of those in power, and grass roots participation is unheard of, professional journalism is consequently viewed with a jaundiced eye—even by the public. Denial of the people's need to know goes back to the Confucius decree that rulers need only inform their subjects of a decision, not give the reason for it. It is only in more recent times that Chinese leaders have deigned to even inform the public after the event. Imparting information to the public is still considered a special favor, not a right.

This then, is the journalistic environment in which the China hand lives and works. The assumption is always that journalists, especially the foreign ones, cause trouble; that their reports are usually irresponsible and a threat to public morals and responsible behavior.

The Chinese tolerate foreign correspondents because they are obliged to reciprocate for their own legions of information gatherers working abroad. They are also accustomed to dealing with the "foreign devils" and in traditional Chinese style attempt to control the relationship with their guests.

This, according to Confucian principle, is done through a system of reciprocity—I scratch your back, you scratch mine. The Chinese treat foreign guests with due deference, respect and generosity and expect the guest to reciprocate by not saying anything unfriendly or critical about the host. This kind of manipulation is as old as China itself and is being applied as assiduously today as it was during the days of the Manchu dynasty.

With this in mind, the late Edgar Snow, the most famous of all the foreign correspondents in China, always insisted on paying his own expenses wherever he went and accepted few favors. (A good policy for journalists to follow at all times anywhere.)

In China, this can be difficult. The foreign journalist is viewed either as friend or foe. Anyone who tries to straddle the middle ground is seen as an opportunist. In the early years after the revolution foreign journalists branded as "enemies" were often placed under house arrest—often for

vv

months at a time. It was a form of isolation that bordered on solitary confinement.

Except for a brief period during the Cultural Revolution, foreign reporters in China have never been censored in the accepted sense of the word. The authorities do however expect self-censorship on pain of denial of travel or outright expulsion.

Good reporters don't knuckle under to this kind of blackmail. The record of the *Globe & Mail*, the newspaper that pioneered post-revolutionary news coverage in China is exemplary. Of its 13 correspondents who have been based in China to date, two have been expelled. Others have been given warnings, one roughed up by the Red Guards, and another accused of being an "international spy."

China, like its neighbor Russia, stands at the crossroads of change. Unlike the friendlier giant next door it has yet to take even the most tentative steps in the direction of democratic reform. Since the Tiananmen Square massacre of 1989, China's leadership has been obsessed with stability and self-preservation. It concedes that its moves towards a market-driven economy must continue, but gradually. The question is, whether the country's geriatric rulers can permit economic change without political reform—whether they can keep the lid on pressure cooker demands for democracy from an impatient younger generation.

No one is watching developments in China more closely and with more at stake than the people of Hong Kong. The British crown colony reverts to Chinese rule in 1997. The apprehension felt by the Hong Kong Chinese is eloquently stated in a *Globe & Mail* interview with a restaurant owner on the island ". . . I think that when the Chinese come, the people of Hong Kong must give up many happinesses." Only time can pass judgment on this pessimistic prophecy.

In the meantime, Beijing has slapped new restrictions on foreign journalists working in China. A 22-point decree issued in 1990 reinforced several rules already on the books and added a few new ones to give authorities wider latitude in warning, banning or expelling correspondents.

The Ministry of Radio, Film and Television, and the Minister of Public Security have also issued regulations requiring anyone owning a satellite dish or planning to get one to secure a license.

Harassment and physical abuse are still a fact of life for correspondents working in China. In 1990, according to the New York-based *Committee to Protect Journalists*, seven foreign correspondents were beaten up by the police, six were detained for questioning and three had film confiscated and/or cameras smashed.

vvv

The entire foreign press corps in China was under severe travel restrictions, with limited or no access to the general public during that year. Hong Kong based reporters were denied entry to the mainland as a matter of course.

Reporters' complaints to the Foreign Ministry Press Section were dismissed as groundless. Their spokesman, Guy Dinmore of *Reuters,* was warned that some foreign reporters were "deliberately . . . trying to jeopardize the social stability and impair the public interests of China."

The main thrust towards democracy in China will not come from the government at the top or the workers, peasants and students at the bottom, but from the new economic and technical class in the middle. This emerging segment of society is an inescapable by-product of a capitalistic economy and one which will not tolerate being disenfranchised for long.

Africa

If, as some critics contend, foreign reporters are guilty of horror-hopping, going from one scene of human tragedy to another, then the continent of Africa provides an abundance of stopovers.

From the Sahel region, pictures of starving, stick-children with swollen stomachs continue to stir a compassionate global response, and shock even the jaded international press corps. South of the Sahara, over a million men, women and children are dying of AIDS, and the World Health Organization predicts that in this decade more than 10 million AIDS-infected children will be born in Africa. Another 10 million will be orphaned, as mothers or both parents succumb to the disease. The paradox is that such an overwhelming and hopeless situation prompts both the public and the media to tune out the story.

WHO's 1990 report on "AIDS in Africa" was given cursory treatment in North American papers, and no mention at all on the national television newscasts.

Political developments are equally discouraging. All over the continent the dream of democracies blossoming out of colonial rule are being shattered and in some cases the dream has turned into a nightmare of inter-tribal violence.

Violence is also being visited with suicidal abandon on the grace, majesty and irreplaceable beauty of Africa's wildlife. And, as the animal populations dwindle, the human generations multiply. Kenya, the centrepiece of nature's East African paradise has the world's highest population growth rate. Its population will double by the end of this decade, and is expected to double again by 2020 for a total of 80 million people. The pressure this will exert on wildlife is incalculable.

vv

Tanzanian statesman Julius Nyerere has warned his people, and the world, that the survival of Africa's wildlife is not just a source of wonder and inspiration, but an integral part of man's livelihood and well-being.

The biggest story on the continent is, and will continue to be, South Africa. The dismantling of apartheid and black vs. black violence will continue to make it a dangerous place to work as the country struggles to solve its seemingly intractable problems.

South Africa's restrictions on reporters imposed under the old state of emergency lifted in 1990 have been replaced by the Declaration of Unrest Areas, a decree which was already on the books. The law does just what the name implies, it keeps correspondents out of areas where the police consider them to be a threat to peace and security.

In 1990, 49 cases of harassment, abuse, detention, threats, woundings, bombings and shootings against journalists were recorded by the *Committee to Protect Journalists* (CPJ). No other country, surveyed came close to that number of incidents.* It must be noted however, that the CPJ survey, while comprehensive, is far from complete.

One experience that didn't make the CPJ report is related by Jonathan Manthorpe, African correspondent for *Southam News*. Manthorpe, Chris Wren of the *New York Times* and Remer Tyson of the *Detroit Free Press* decided to attend a rally of the South African Conservative Party at the Voortrekker Monument—shrine of Afrikanerdom in Pretoria. They were joined by Jerelyn Eddings, newly appointed South Africa correspondent for the *Baltimore Sun*, and Sylvia Vollenhoven, who writes for a Swedish newspaper. The ugly incident which ensued wouldn't have happened except for one thing—the two women reporters were not white. Eddings is a black American, Vollenhoven is, under South Africa's race laws, "Cape Colored."

Manthorpe recalls how the glint of hardness was clearly evident in the blue eyes of the young flaxen-haired girls handing out pamphlets at the entrance points.

As the four young correspondents approached a fence overlooking the amphitheatre a rock whizzed past. They were confronted by a man carrying the old Transvaal flag demanding to know why they were there. Stumped by the official press cards he was shown, he angrily left.

It soon became apparent that the rally had been hijacked by the extreme right. Swastika-like flags and other paraphernalia prevalent during rallies in Nazi Germany were everywhere. Some men carried guns or pistols in

* In Africa, Sudan and Kenya came in second, each recording 25 cases of abuse.

vvv

their pockets. Wren and Tyson were grabbed from behind by two burly men and frog-marched into a nearby bush. Explanations that the two black women were foreign correspondents invited to the rally by the Conservative Party itself were of no avail.

"Skiet, skiet," one of the men shouted. "Shoot them, shoot them."

Within seconds, two police officers emerged from the bushes to rescue the reporters. The beer was starting to flow and the police couldn't guarantee their safety. "You should leave," said one of the policemen. "It's just like a red flag to a bull, those two," he went on, pointing to the two black women.

Manthorpe says they were standing beside their cars debating the next move when a Mercedes Benz pulled up, the driver in serious conversation on a cellular phone. Being shot at on a highway is not unheard of in South Africa, so the reporters decided to call it a day. They gave the Mercedes the slip and headed back to safety.

White reporters venturing into black areas have gotten themselves into similar predicaments. The incidents are graphic illustrations of how dangerous reporting in South Africa can be.

Local reporters in black African states don't have an easy time of it either. The master press plan for newly-independent African states enunciated in the sixties by Ghana's Kwame Nkrumah is still followed.

> The necessity for a clear ideology of the African Revolution must be to view problems in the right perspective so that they (journalists) can write about them with insight and understanding. The drumbeat of the African Revolution must throb in the pages of his newspapers and magazines, it must sound in the voices and feelings of our news readers. To this end, we need a new kind of journalist of the African Revolution.

Nkrumah's dictum, like Lenin's before him, did not tolerate a critical press, which these men viewed as an obstruction to revolutionary progress just a surely as subversion and armed insurrection.

Nothing much has changed since their time. Recently the *Ghanaian Times* was forced to drop a series of articles critical of the government. A *Ghana Broadcasting Corporation* producer was required to pay all costs, including air time, of a program he produced about a businessman. Speculation by the businessman represents opposition to state-owned agricultural enterprises. In another case of press repression, soldiers visited the home of a columnist and warned him to stop writing articles critical of the government and the army.

In Zambia, all government media are prohibited from reporting on activities of the political opposition.

vvv

In Zimbabwe, any attempt by journalists to investigate alleged conflict of interest by elected politicians invariably results in physical threats, firings or both.

In Kenya, non-government news conferences are routinely broken up by the police.

It is a repressive atmosphere that is not conducive to effective reporting by foreign or domestic correspondents. Canadians are, however, generally given preferential treatment over other foreign reporters in black African countries as well as other developing states throughout the world. They are beneficiaries of the trust and goodwill Canada has built up through its international aid programs and support for the Third World at the United Nations and through the Commonwealth.

Africa nevertheless gets scant attention in the Canadian and international press. The primary reason is its lack of global political and economic clout. It deserves better. As it did for Henry Stanley of the *New York Herald* when he penetrated its mysterious depths to find Dr. David Livingstone a hundred years ago, the African continent continues to intrigue, inspire and to haunt.

Latin America

"How much do you charge to kill someone?"

"Anywhere from five to ten dollars, depends on who they are. To kill you, an American journalist, fifteen dollars."

Youthful bravado? Perhaps. But nevertheless that chilling conversation took place recently during a TV interview between a teenager in Bogota, Colombia and an American female journalist.

Colombia is the world's most dangerous beat. It is a country where journalists wear bulletproof vests and take the precaution of looking under their cars for bombs before they leave for work. It has the highest incidence of kidnapping, murder and torture of journalists in the world. Since 1980, 46 have been assassinated, seven in one 10 week period in 1991.

Any reporter who risks doing a story on the drug cartel, or the leftist guerillas, runs a better-than-even chance of being kidnapped or killed. Domestic reporters are the main target, but foreign reporters are also in constant danger.

West German reporter Hero Buss was kidnapped by one of the drug cartels when he tried to interview a leftist guerila leader. He was released after being held for several months. Sylvia Duzan wasn't so lucky. The British Channel 4 reporter was gunned down and killed along with three

vvv

peasant leaders while investigating paramilitary troops in the pay of drug lords.

Correspondents assigned to Colombia and many other areas of Latin America live and work in an atmosphere of hate, violence and death. Life is of little or no value. In Colombia alone, more than 3 000 people with no known identity are buried in mass graves every year. Street crimes, and assassinations carried out for a few dollars, claim most of these nameless dead.

Peru and Brazil have also become risky assignment areas. The threat to foreign news services in Peru comes primarily from the leftist Shining Path guerrillas who hijack agency offices and force them to disseminate political messages. Recent targets have included Germany's DPA and United Press International. (Most of these attacks are aimed at local radio and TV stations which are temporarily captured and used for propaganda broadcasts.)

In Brazil, attacks on the media come mainly from the police. Articles about alleged police or political corruption as often as not result in bomb threats, police raids on news offices, crippling libel suits and death threats.

Reprisals against foreign correspondents are less harsh, but police harassment can make it difficult to do a story properly. A four-man ABC *Nightline* crew was detained for several hours on the trumped up excuse that the Americans were involved with kidnappers in the area. They were in fact working on a story about police torture in Brazil.

The litany of attacks on the press in Latin America seems endless even against correspondents working for the foreign media.

Maria Laura Avignolo of France's *Liberation* was threatened with death for an article appearing in *Paris Match* (all of which she did not write) about Argentine President Carlos Saul Menem. Menem, himself an avowed democrat, threatened to file a libel suit against Avignolo, claiming she had maligned his name internationally.

In Chile, British reporter Jonathan Moyle was found dead in a hotel closet. Police dismissed his death as a suicide, but later evidence pointed to murder. Speculation is, Moyle was killed because he had uncovered information about a Chilean arms dealer and the Iraqi government. There were 26 other cases of media abuse in Chile recorded in 1990 by the *Committee to Protect Journalists.*

(Such illustrious democracies as Canada, Britain, Australia and France did not escape the CPJ's attention. But alleged fractions were not of a serious nature.)

It's a short walk across the bridge connecting California and Mexico at Tijuana. Yet it's another world—a hostile world where human rights

vvv

and the environment are recklessly abused and corruption is endemic. Says NBC's Tom Brokaw, "when you start taking press freedom for granted, just make that short drive from San Diego to Tijuana."

Mexico is under pressure from both Washington and Ottawa to clean up its environmental and drug image as part of any future North American Free Trade Agreement. Yet little if anything is ever said by these governments about journalists, both domestic and foreign, who are threatened, maimed and murdered in Mexico as a matter of course simply because their reports are critical of the government.

"There was a time," says Eduardo Valle, president of the Union of Democratic Journalists, "when there were three untouchables in Mexico—the President, the military and our patron saint, the Virgin of Guadalupe. We have had to add drug traffickers and the police to that list."

The police are as much feared by reporters as the drug gangs. In fact they are often one and the same thing. Says writer Amparo Davila, "An outspoken journalist is at the mercy of a venal judge, an eager-to-please policeman, a threatened drug lord. It's part of our lives."

Over a four-year period between 1988-91, 17 Mexican journalists were killed—either by drug cartels, government officials or the police.

These disturbing statistics don't seem to bother trade negotiators in Washington and Ottawa. Simon Reisman, chief Canadian architect of the U.S.-Canada free trade pact, encouraged the Mexicans to get on with a trilateral North American deal saying Mexicans shouldn't wait to sort out all their problems before signing up. Waiting, says Reisman, just creates more problems.

Journalists don't agree. And if, as one Mexican reporter suggests, the Mexican government "is more sensitive to criticism in English than in Spanish," then the onus is on the foreign correspondent to do the job in a country where deadlines can be interpreted quite literally.

As memories of the cold war fade, foreign reporters must learn to deal with a new kind of global story—ethnic and tribal conflicts. These are breaking out in every part of the world, as distinct societal and national groupings struggle to free themselves from what they consider to be artificial and in many cases forced political and economic unions.

The greatest potential for violence and global destabilization comes from the newly independent republics of the old USSR where Lithuania, Latvia and Estonia are already fully independent and Moldova, Armenia and Ukraine, among others, are more or less going their own way within the new commonwealth.

The same phenomena are occurring in India, Sri Lanka, Ethiopia, Yugoslavia, The Middle East, and even in Canada, where Quebec appears to be moving inexorably towards some form of sovereignty association or outright independence.

Like Chinese boxes these nationalist movements, if they succeed, will discover smaller nationalist movements within themselves. Will Quebec grant its Cree and Mohawk nations the same sovereignty it seeks for itself from Canada? Could an independent Georgia in turn grant independence to the nationalist groups within its borders who do not want to be governed from either Moscow or Tbilisi? Tribalism is on the rise throughout the world, making the foreign reporter's job more complex, more unpredictable and much more dangerous.

Japan

The foreign journalist's job in Japan is equally complex even though there's little danger of political upheaval, nor are there threats to correspondents' safety.

At first glance there is little to differentiate Japan from a Western country. There are office towers, freeways, department stores and malls crowded with modishly dressed shoppers. In this instance though, looks are definitely deceiving. Of all the world's cultures none is more different from that of the West than Japan's.

A Japanese-American businessman puts it this way, "It's like looking at two flower beds. Both appear the same with colorful blossoms, leaves and stems. Yet, if you remove the earth, there, under a common exterior lies a totally unique root system." It is this complex cultural structure that continues to confound politicians, businessmen and journalists.

No one finds the Japanese more perplexing than the Americans, with WW II still deeply ingrained in their psyche. They thought that after their military conquest of Japan they had succeeded in reshaping the country in their own image. They had after all given their former enemy a democratic constitution, revamped Japan's educational system, introduced the principles of Western business management and helped turn "Made in Japan" from a label of derision to one of international respect.

Nevertheless, stereotypes propagated during the war continue to linger and most of these images are negative—ant-like conformity, female submissiveness, workers who are mere cogs in a huge corporate machine, and so on. These images are part caricature and part reality. Unfortunately, the news media have emphasized caricature at the expense of accuracy.

Correspondents may not be entirely at fault. Patrick Smith, writing in *The New Yorker*, points out that in Japan symbols can easily be mistaken for substance because the Japanese themselves often fail to differentiate

vv

between the two. This, as much as anything else, contributes to the opaque picture we have of the country and its people.

The Japanese, says Smith, do not put the high value on winning that we do in the West. (International business is a notable exception.) Americans who have played professional baseball in Japan say spectators are happiest when the game ends in a tie. Both sides are winners. No one has lost face. It's the *asobi* mentality at work in which playing the game to one's best ability is more important than winning.

Business is something else. Flooding North American and European markets with underpriced products is fair game even if it hurts Japan's key trading partners. Here, another philosophy comes into play; preserving the essence of Japanese culture while at the same time taking advantage of what the outside world has to offer.

In recent years, journalists have begun to take these subtleties into account and forgo stereotypes in favor of substantive subjects. These have included education (Japan's defeat in WW II is barely mentioned in the curriculum), work (16-hour days, six days a week for male office workers are not uncommon), and the second class status of women (men don't want to marry those over 25).

Almost without exception the information Canadians get about Japan comes from American sources. Most Canadian media owners find the cost of maintaining a bureau in Tokyo prohibitive. The handful of bureaus in place are in danger of being shut down because of exorbitant costs. The Canadian news consumer is the loser. If Japan changes, it will be a major news story. If it doesn't change, it will be an even bigger story.

For correspondents on the ground the one overriding issue will be whether Japan, the economic super power will become Japan the political and military power. Of equal importance is Tokyo's will, or lack of it, to institute fair trading and environmental practices. With the sole exception of the Sony Corporation, big business still seems oblivious or uncaring about the poor image it projects abroad. Sony executives are calling for shorter working hours and higher pay to bring the cost of Japanese exports into line with international standards. So far, the move hasn't gone down well in the executive suites of Japan Inc.

The force that ultimately pushes the country toward change may well lie with the *shinjinrui*, the generation spanning the mid-teens to the mid-twenties. Their values represent a sharp departure from that of their parents. They are voracious consumers, not savers, refuse to dedicate their lives to the company, travel abroad and value individually over group mentality. How the "Japan story" unfolds in the years ahead will depend on whether the *shinjinrui* turn out to be a generation of genuine reformers or merely part of the normal generational gap.

Back To The Future—Live

> We are in the 'good grief Martha, look what's happening on TV now' era of journalism.
> — Edwin Diamond, Media Critic New York Magazine

ANYONE OLD ENOUGH TO REMEMBER THE EARLY YEARS of live television will recall that half the fun was catching all the bloopers. Videotape was still years away in the late forties and early fifties and high cost film was reserved almost exclusively for news and public affairs programs. Once on the air, there was no going back on shows like Sid Caesar, Uncle Miltie (Berle), General Electric Theatre and Your Hit Parade. Except for the canned applause they went live from start to finish. There were no retakes, no dubbing, no cosmetic editing or mid-show script changes.

The gaffes were, as might be expected, frequent and memorable. Phones were answered before they rang, door knobs came off in actors' hands leaving them no alternative but to hastily exit through an adjacent open window. Dialogue carefully crafted by scriptwriters ended up being ad libbed. Producers' blood pressure dropped dramatically with the long awaited introduction of videotape which allowed them to package shows and retake scenes until they met acceptable standards.

Videotape was also eventually adapted for compact portable news cameras. Temperamental and unpredictable 16 mm film cameras and sound gear were junked in favor of high quality ENG (electronic news gathering) mini cams that offer instant playback. Sequences that don't come off can be shot again. Eliminated too is the heartbreak of seeing an entire day's shooting ruined in the film processing "soup." Video tape is a godsend for reporters. No fuss, no mess, quickly and cleanly electronically edited with little or no risk of losing the picture.

The next step was getting the story to air without wasting critical time fighting traffic getting the tape from assignment location to the studio. Again technology sprang to the rescue in the form of the mobile transmission van with a dish on the roof to beam pictures directly back to the newsroom a few miles away.

The juggernaut of technical advance didn't stop there. Satellite dishes became more compact, more portable and global in reach. The television correspondent evolved into a virtual one man uplink not unlike the *Saturday Night Live* spoof in which a character with a satellite dish

vvv

attached to his helmet, backpack stuffed with gear, plays the role of an electronic roving reporter.

The fact is, caricature is no longer that far removed from reality. As competition heats up, getting the sensational story first, at all costs, has become an obsession with editors and producers. Often the best way of beating the competition is to go live.

In the headlong technological race to perfect the how of communications, television is forgetting that the most important part of news is the what of a story. And that's where the flesh and blood dimension of the correspondent comes in.

In the mad dash to keep up with technology, the reporter is losing "think time" which has been scarce at the best of times. Back in the misty days of film, reporters had a breathing space while the crew travelled from the assignment location to the lab and ran the film through the processor. This could take anywhere from one to two hours, giving the reporter time to gather his or her thoughts, think about content, check uncertain facts, shape the story line, write and voice the script. Even with that amount of time, stories often made it to air with seconds to spare.

ENG has cut even deeper into shrinking preparation time. Direct transmission from the mobile vans and the elimination of lab processing means the reporter has virtually no time left to organize the facts, decide on the lead, extract the right sound bite and generally create a cohesive, insightful story that contains all the elements of good reporting.

Speeded-up technology is putting a great deal of emphasis on glib performance at the expense of thoughtful content. The swing towards the exploitation of the drama and the immediacy of live news has reduced think time to near zero. The question asked in local newsrooms is often not what's going on, but where can we go live tonight?

Ratings driven producers have regrettably reverted to the old ambulance and fire truck chasing mentality in the hopes of going live with a slice of human tragedy for the sole purpose of catering to viewers with *National Enquirer* tastes. A family watching in horror as their house goes up in flames, a distraught young man threatening to jump to his death from a bridge, or the gruesome aftermath of a car crash are all grist for the go live news mill.

The fuel that propels live television is *dramatic imagery*. This was most spectacularly illustrated during the 1992 Los Angeles race riots. So was the medium's most glaring shortcoming of all—its inability to show more than one screen-sized bite of what is going on at any given time.

Los Angeles television gave viewers reporters standing on debris-littered street corners able to show only what was happening within the camera's limited periphery. To sustain visual interest, directors called for

vvv

endless shots of shattering glass and looters dragging their booty from wrecked stores. Such coverage encouraged hundreds of others to leave their TV sets to join the smash-and-grab frenzy.

To TV's credit, the live pictures no doubt saved the life of Reginald Denny. Several black residents living near an intersection over which a TV news helicopter was hovering were shocked to see the white truck driver dragged from his cab and being beaten to a bloody pulp by black gang members. At considerable risk to their own safety, they rushed to the scene and drove Denny to a hospital.

Camera-laden choppers also zoomed in on burning buildings giving the erroneous impression that the entire California metropolis was in flames. It was TV in the raw, substituting imagery for reality. Yet no station dared shut down the cameras to bring the story into some kind of focus and perspective for fear of missing some sensational shot.

Anchor desks did push field reporters for the "big picture" from time to time, but they were asking the wrong people. Reporters on the spot don't have the vaguest idea of how the story as a whole is unfolding. Their job is to provide the desk with a snapshot picture of what is happening on that particular corner. They have little or no opportunity to question anyone in a position to put events into some kind of comprehensive whole.

Responsible journalism calls for a process of deliberate selection of information. The technology of live television news has swept aside that basic tenet of the profession to turn the reporter and the camera into a participant of the event rather than remaining the impartial observer.

Inevitably the technological breakthroughs in international satellite transmissions brought the world of live television with all its editorial ramifications to the foreign correspondent beat, catching reporters unprepared for its relentless demands.

If reporters working abroad had any illusions that they were in control of the new technology—that it was not about to dictate their coverage they were jolted into reality at Dhahran and Tel Aviv during the Gulf War. The demands of those stories showed that journalism has a long way to go before it catches up with technology. The push of a button (albeit an expensive push) in New York, London or Toronto brought up the voice and image of correspondents in Riyadh, Tel Aviv and even in bomb-ravaged Baghdad when generators could squeeze out enough power. The sights and sounds were brought to the home screen, but so was confusion and a lack of factual information. The instant access meant the editorial process was being conducted live on the go in front of millions of viewers.

vvv

Reports went like this: "Our information is that five missiles have landed in Tel Aviv at least some with chemical warheads." A few minutes later, "Reliable military sources now say none of the scuds carried chemical warheads, all were conventionally armed." Correspondents, on the urging of anchormen at home, fumbled with gas masks, treating the audience to the bizarre sight of a reporter peering through the goggles dramatically delivering barely audible reports of chemical attacks that never happened. In fairness to the reporters, they could not be sure at the time that they weren't under chemical attack. It is known, however, that at least some reporters used the masks for dramatic effect.

Another reporter witnessed military jets taking off from a Tel Aviv air base and immediately reported that the planes were on their way to Iraq to retaliate for the scud attacks. As it turned out Israel never did retaliate.

The same Keystone Cops comedy was being played out in Saudi Arabia where one on-air correspondent panicked everyone within earshot by yelling "gas—I smell gas." The "gas" turned out to be exhaust fumes from the jets taking off from the Dhahran air base.

The scud/patriot missile contest also generated mass confusion.

"All scuds were intercepted by patriot missiles," one correspondent confidently assured viewers. Then, the inevitable correction a few minutes later. "Our information now is that apparently two did get through." And so it went. There was little opportunity to check or verify. Once in front of a live camera, the correspondent had no choice but to stay put and report only on what was within his visual range or what someone was whispering from off camera. Unlike election night coverage or a political

vv

convention, there was no stack of notes and clippings to fall back on, no army of researchers behind the scenes feeding in reliable information, nor the opportunity to "throw" to other correspondents.

Live transmissions kept the military nervous, the public in the dark a good deal of the time and reporters scrambling for something credible to report. Anchormen editorialized on air to fill time, and in the process asked thoughtless questions. Correspondents were at times hard pressed to adhere to a cardinal rule of broadcasting—that no matter what kind of a question you're thrown by the anchor, you must never make him look stupid. After all, he's being paid millions to look and sound like the most intelligent human being on earth and networks don't appreciate correspondents who shatter that illusion.*

The CBC's Brian Stewart, who reported out of Dhahran, was able to observe first-hand the more flush American networks going live at the drop of a scud.

Says Stewart, "I noticed that some of these stand ups in the middle of the night were a bit like dangling someone by their heels over Niagara Falls and saying, 'give me a feel for what you're feeling right now'."

In live coverage much revolves around feeling and experience. The reporter is nailed to one spot for long periods of time with no way of getting away to check facts or gather new information on a story that is changing by the minute.

"We are in a constant battle with our producers on this," says Charles Bierbauer, Senior White House correspondent for CNN. "Their big fault," he goes on to say, "is that they want you standing in front of the cameras telling news all the time when you have no time to get at it."

There are those who suggest that the "live and be damned" syndrome has to be broken, that news organizations have a responsibility to curb the public's appetite for raw-as-it-happens news. News coverage, it is argued, has to be more than a tower of Babel—or a global town hall meeting. But it's too late. The genie is out of the bottle. The ratings game, and in some cases responsible journalism, demands live television.

---

* The late Steve Rowan found that out the hard way. During live coverage of a space shot, anchorman Walter Cronkite commented that the brightly lit space centre in Houston, visible behind Rowan, surely indicated that everyone at the space centre was working late into the night preparing for the launch. "No," the outspoken Saskatchewanian replied, "everyone's gone home. Those lights are on because the cleaning ladies are hard at work." Whatever the reason, Steve's career with CBS was brief.

vvv

"Imagine this scenario for a moment," says CBC anchor Peter Mansbridge. "It is 1963, a news bulletin is read on air saying 'Something has happened in Dallas. We are not sure what, but Lyndon Johnson is a name you should perhaps get used to. More details at 6:30 tonight'."

The Kennedy assassination was, indeed, one of those events that absolutely demanded going live. The public wanted to know what had happened, what reporters knew or thought they knew and if mistakes were made that had to be corrected on the air, that was quite understandable and acceptable. The important thing was to talk about it; to participate in a kind of mass therapy by going through this catharsis together. Anything except the unbearable pain of suffering in silence.

As technology makes it easier for television to go live from virtually any spot on earth, this kind of participatory television news will continue to grow and be abused. Accuracy will, to a large extent, be sacrificed at the altar of immediacy and drama. Journalists of the old 'get it first but first get it right school' are fighting a losing battle against the trend to go live, often for the simple reason that the technology is there.

Networks and individual stations will continue to do so primarily out of fear that if they don't the competition will and because viewers have become more tolerant of mistakes.

"The public is easygoing, perhaps too easygoing about this," says Michael Arlen of *The New Yorker*. "But," he says, "if a TV organization hires responsible people trying to do a serious job—they'll make mistakes, sure—everybody makes mistakes, but the public is tolerant and wants to be involved."

Even government leaders responsible for initiating televised events in the first place disconcertingly become part of the participatory process. When all hell was breaking loose over Baghdad on the first day of the Gulf War, world leaders from the Secretary General of the United Nations to American Secretary of Defense Dick Cheney to President Bush himself were glued to their TV sets as allied bombers turned the Iraq capital into a gigantic fireworks display. Television was bringing the news to the White House faster than the president could get it from his generals in the field, prompting Bush's rather scary comment, "I only know what you know. I'm watching CNN too."

Live news telecasting calls for a new attitude, not just on the part of the public but most importantly by the broadcasters themselves. Besides practising restraint, journalists will have to be more forthcoming with their audience and learn to say "I don't know" when they're not in possession of the facts. That's not easy for a reporter to do. After all, he or she is paid to know. Nevertheless it will have to happen because the public can quickly figure out whether or not it's being scammed.

vv

Rational decisions must be made to adjust to circumstances that change by the minute. Cool heads will be required to avoid the temptation to jump on the first piece of information that comes down the pike. If the live coverage during the Gulf War taught correspondents anything it was to stay calm and not become wired to the point of short-circuiting in a confusing mix of contradicting information in which rumors are reported as such, repeated by another reporter as unconfirmed information, only to rebound on the originator minutes later as a self-created "hard fact." The whole exercise turns into nothing more than an incestuous feeding frenzy for a news-starved anchor desk.

Mistakes and faulty information are inherent factors in live news reporting. No matter how assiduously correspondents and producers try to avoid them, they're going to happen. Silent phones will be answered and door knobs will come off jammed doors. But unlike the escape afforded the pioneer actors of live television, there's no nearby window waiting for the correspondent from which to make a quick exit.

Personal Perspectives

My career has led me to encounter in all stages of sobriety and sanity, presidents and prime ministers, monarchs and mountebanks, heroes and rogues.

— Drew Middleton

IT IS 7:30 IN THE MORNING. BRIGHT SUNLIGHT IS STREAM-ing through the tattered white lace curtains. The cracked oil painting of the old man driving a team of oxen along a tree-lined country lane slowly comes into focus. The curtains, the painting, the yellowing white walls could be a room in any one of a thousand seedy East European hotels. And the smell. Must be Sverdlovsk. A Siberian blizzard has forced us to overnight at a rickety old hotel near the airport. The air in my room is diffused with the odor of urine standing in a congealing pool on the bathroom floor. The slant of the tiles towards the bathtub allows me just enough dry space to use the sink. Saved by shoddy Soviet workmanship.

But those massive oak sliding doors separating my room from the one adjoining—it can't be Sverdlovsk. Ah yes! The big sliding wooden doors—reminders of a grander era when they opened up from the bed chamber, of which I was the current occupant, into the drawing room of a spacious hotel suite. Nineteenth century elegance had long ago succumbed to twentieth century socialist expediency. The beautifully finished hand-carved doors had been rudely bolted together. Voila! Two rooms. More tourist dollars. Never mind that you can hear the striking of a match next door.

Noise behind those wooden sliding doors. Thumping noises. Moans followed by muffled dialogue between a man and a woman—sounds like German. Probably East German tourists. The words become louder and accusatory. There are sounds of dressing, the clink of change and keys.

"That's all you wanted, wasn't it?" The woman's voice is hurt and plaintive.

"So, what did you expect, a promise of marriage after the first night?"

"No, but why do you have to rush off like this?"

"Because I want to, that's why."

"Will I see you tomorrow?"

"Who knows. Maybe. We'll see."

With that, the click of the room's hallway door.

vv

As if on cue, the woman breaks into hysterical sobs which soon segue into a loud rhythmical snoring. I lie on my back staring at the antiquated light fixture above my bed. I'm wide awake. The planned events of the day soon to dawn churn in my mind. Camera crew shoots presidential motorcade arriving city centre from airport. Richard Nixon making unprecedented visits to Bucharest.

I must have fallen back to sleep, because here I am in the same room with those sliding doors. But, the smell! That wasn't there last night. I feel as though I'm being gassed. The bathroom is enveloped in a blue haze. I step outside into the hall. A maid in the corridor assures me I'll live—just fumigating to keep the cockroach population in check. Fat chance. The repulsive little creatures have been around longer than man and will be here long after man has disappeared off the face of the earth. Even Stalin couldn't liquidate them. Ceausescu won't have any luck either.

Back to the bathroom. I open my shaving kit. Two plump reddish brown cockroaches dash out from under the red-and-white Colgate toothpaste tube and scamper for refuge behind the sink. I'm mildly consoled by the thought that they don't bite like the bed bugs in Leningrad, leaving tiny red welts on the skin. Breathing shallowly, I shower, shave and dress in record time. I'm off to have breakfast with my camera crew around the huge disintegrating Lido Hotel swimming pool. The tile work and masonry is crumbling, but a big thumping engine, located somewhere in the bowels of the old building, still turns the gigantic paddles of the wave machine that must have thrilled the children of the wealthy European tourists who frequented the Lido to sample the delights of Bucharest in better days.

Revived by the fresh air, the lapping of the pseudo waves and several cups of muddy Turkish coffee, we prepare for the day's work. Soundman Rick Hunt, just back from Vietnam where he collected several shrapnel scars, helps cameraman Phil Pendry get the gear together. I'm off to co-ordinate the day's shooting with my Romanian translator/minder whose stock answer to every request is: "that is probably possible only in principle." Another day of reporting from Eastern Europe has begun.

Romania, Mozambique, Somalia, Iraq, the old Soviet republics, Burma, Guatemala—the locales may change, but with minor twists, the scenarios are the same. To handle them, the job requires stamina, both mental and physical. It can be exciting and lonely. Long periods on the road, in and out of hotels; arguments with rude airport staff and surly government bureaucrats speaking all kinds of incomprehensible languages, including English; sorting out change from half a dozen countries as you fumble for the taxi driver's tip.

vvv

Would-be correspondents who expect a riproaring sex life on the road will be disappointed, unless they want to buy it on the street. From my experience, even the most libidinous of my colleagues crashed into bed alone from exhaustion after a frustrating day of dealing with local bureaucrats, officious guards, flight schedules, non-existent hotel reservations and unsympathetic assignment editors back home. One female reporter once confided to me that she worked as a team with her cameraman both on the job and off. Such "in house" arrangements may have worked for some, but an American colleague of mine summed it up succinctly if rather indelicately: "getting laid and getting the story are mutually exclusive. You get one or the other but not both."

There are of course exceptions to the rules. When I was in Moscow, an American reporter friend phoned me up early one morning to inform me that there had been an assassination attempt on Brezhnev the previous afternoon as a cosmonauts' motorcade drove from the airport to the Kremlin.

"Where did you get that from?" I asked.

"It's all over town," he answered. "My date told me this morning when she got out of bed to look for some cigarettes."

Time was, when reporters were posted to say Rome, London or Tokyo, they didn't stray too far from base. The Rome reporter reported on Italy, the Paris reporter on France and so on. Today, the Paris reporter is likely to be anywhere but Paris. I remember Peter Jennings telling me when he was based in London for ABC, that he spent more time in Cairo and Beirut than in London. Routing satellite transmissions allow editors to view the world as a giant chessboard and foreign correspondents as pieces to be moved from place to place. My notes for a three-month period during my Moscow posting illustrate the peripatetic lifestyle of today's foreign correspondent.

> *Rome in August*. They call it the Eternal City. Good name. Feels like the place has been here forever and will be here for a thousand years from now. The NATO foreign ministers' conference opens Monday. Must somehow contact the Canadian delegation, talk to Mitchell Sharp's exec to find out what position Canada taking re: Warsaw Pact's pitch for European Security Conference.

> *Sunday*. Up at day break. Can hardly believe this is Rome. No traffic to speak of. Streets empty. Wandered over to the Coliseum. No tourists yet. Sat on stone slab opposite the royal box where the Caesars' thumbs up or thumbs down determined the fate of vanquished gladiators. Tomorrow, discussion will revolve around two superpowers whose rulers share the thumbs up or down power over the lives of the earth's inhabitants. Power the Roman Caesars couldn't even dream about. The massive stone floor on

vv

which Christians were thrown to the lions have long since caved into the dungeons below, which housed the lions' cages and the luckless human participants of these ancient spectacles. Overgrown with weeds, it has become home to a multitude of cats of infinite colors, shapes, sizes and temperaments.

The morning sun peers through a gaping rock-hewn window cut out of the rounded wall, as it has hundreds of thousands of times before. Jolted from my reverie by an intense sustained chatter, I look through the "window" to see a group of Japanese tourists more intent on nattering among themselves than hearing what their Italian guide has to say about ancient Rome.

Radio feeds from NATO meeting site on outskirts of city chaotic. Elderly chap in charge of booking radio lines looks as though he worked with Marconi on the world's first radio receiver. He's totally baffled by the fact that Canada isn't a part of the United States, and by the number of broadcast networks in North America.

"Here we have one," he tells me. "You have Chee Bee Es, Eh Bee Chee, En Bee Chee—now you comma wit Chee Bee Chee." He slaps the palm of his hand on his forehead in disgust and starts dialling for yet another line to North America.

Next stop Bucharest. U.S. President Nixon due here in a few days for a brief stop on his global tour. Americans cosying up to Ceausescu (as we are) not because they like him or because he's not a communist but because he won't kow tow to Moscow—Nixon's way of irritating the Russian bear. American press corps travelling with Nixon are a testy bunch, they spend half the press briefings yelling and shouting at each other, American journalists again prove themselves to be the rudest but best reporters. Staying on in Bucharest. Mitchell Sharp our External Affairs Minister here for a few days. Also exploiting Ceausescu's independent line from Moscow. Main interest is trade, specifically selling Romania Candu nuclear power plant. Romanians hit up Canadians for a bit of charity. Danube River is in full flood in northeastern corner of the country. No crops, heavy damage. Canada promising wheat shipments. Tomorrow my CBC film crew from Paris and I off to Galati and Braila to see devastation.

Next stop, Belgrade Yugoslavia. Another communist country going its own way without direction from Moscow—"coke communism," they call it. The External Affairs Minister visited Marshall Tito today in Beograd Castle. The last survivor of the WW II leaders consented to a photo session. He's a striking figure even in a charcoal-grey business suit. His ample ruddy face is

vvv

topped off by a thinning head of carefully combed red hair. (Poor dye job, I thought.)

Smoking a stogie, Tito bantered easily with the Canadian press contingent. Sharp ordered a drink of Canadian rye. Tito preferred brandy. "Ever try Canadian whiskey?" Sharp asked. "Yes," Tito replied, "I tried it (pause) once."

September—The West German election campaign in full swing. Toronto suggests not worth while going back to Moscow home base and suggest I head for Bonn—CBC London crew will be waiting there. Neo-Nazi party fielding slate of candidates under Theodore Von Thadden. Will be test of far right political sentiment in Germany. Not getting much on the air, but election campaign is giving me a chance to see West Germany. Neo-Nazi rallies, especially in Nuremburg violent. Getting used to police water cannon.

Met Willy Brandt today standing on tarmac of Cologne—Bonn International Airport, waiting for flight to Washington in his capacity as foreign minister of current coalition government. This doesn't keep him form also running for the chancellorship against his boss, the current chancellor. German politics takes some getting used to.

October—German elections over. Willy Brandt is new chancellor. The neo-Nazis wiped out. Checking out few additional stories for CBC current affairs producers while I'm here. Trying to get interviews with Albert Speer, Hitler's armaments and supply minister who has just published his memoirs. Initial response positive, but suspect big bucks involved. Doubt if the Corp will go for it.

Late October—Back in Moscow. Haven't seen the kids in nearly three months. Beautiful Russian autumn. Russians going through fall ritual of picking mushrooms in the forests around Moscow. Need a break badly and CBC agrees. Dona and I leave for Helsinki Wednesday for a week of R and R.

Travelling assignments stretching from days into weeks and weeks into months go with the correspondent's territory. In one eight-month period, NBC's Arthur Kent covered the Tiananmen Square massacre in Beijing, the collapse of communism in several East European countries, the Berlin wall coming down, the bloody revolution in Romania and the continuing war in Afghanistan. Kent's peripatetic lifestyle prompted anchorman Tom Brokaw to comment, "Arthur's been everywhere but home."

Such real-life drama and adventure (with occasional glamor) exact a heavy price. A normal social and home life does not exist. The job comes

vvv

first. Spouses and children too often take a back seat with the result that the divorce rate among reporters is among the highest of any profession.

The demands of news gathering, domestic pressure and lack of social life lead too many reporters to drink. Knowlton Nash, my counterpart in Washington for many years, says some of our colleagues drank out of guilt, some for comradeship but also out of fear. "Fear that someone would beat us to a story—failure to meet high demands of themselves and actual performance. A few slid into alcoholism."

To this could be added the constant pressure, especially on younger reporters, to be accepted as professional equals by their peers. The fraternity does not warm readily to newcomers. "New boys" have to prove themselves before acceptance in the cosy circle of the "good ol' boys." Breaking in isn't easy. The newcomer is usually an unknown quantity. Sources who speak freely to veteran reporters are guarded with newcomers while they take the measure of the new kid on the block. In the best of circumstances the novice reporter works harder and more imaginatively to please his editors and peers. In dangerous situations the new reporter often sets out to make a mark by taking stupid chances. (The consequences of this are detailed in the chapter "Cloaks, Daggers, and Trench Coats.")

Besides dodging bullets and bombs, the international roving reporter has to reckon with the threat of illness. Once off the beaten path, a small survival kit is a must; it should include items like antiseptic cream, diarrhea cure, water purification tablets, dried foods, etc.

No book on foreign correspondents would be complete without reference to the finer points of preparing expense accounts. Among my colleagues it was taken as an article of faith that anyone could be a reporter but only those who had mastered the art of submitting a well-padded, watertight expense return qualified as a foreign correspondent.

Everyone fiddled the expense claims, some more than others. We frankly didn't see anything dishonest about it. After every assignment, even the most parsimonious among us were money out of pocket. There are the dozens of little extras that have to be bought before and during any trip, not to mention that one round of drinks in a European bar can knock a fair-sized hole in a hundred dollar bill. One meal in a good restaurant usually demolished the per diem designed by some conscientious budget committee to last a full day. So, we thought, some kind of rough justice was called for to save us from personal financial ruin.

The accountants normally scanned our returns with a tolerant eye. The more imaginative items submitted by the worst offenders were somewhat more carefully scrutinized. After returning from assignment in South America a CBC colleague of mine had one of his expense account entries

vv

red pencilled. Listing piranha repellent as an expense was pushing it a bit too far even for our normally indulgent news office accountant.

I was never very good at the game, but I did learn a few tricks—mostly nickel and dime stuff. One was avoiding the front seat when sharing a taxi with two or three other reporters. The person sitting next to the driver always gets stuck with the tab, but you can bet your beat-up trench coat that every guy in the back seat included the taxi fare on his expense account.

If expense account artists were rated on a scale of 1-10, I'd probably end up with a 5—maybe a 6 in a good year. The fellow who came up with the piranha repellent was a definite 10.

There's a general misconception among the public that foreign correspondents speak several languages and spend a great deal of time studying international affairs. Sadly this is not the case. When I was posted to Moscow, the CBC gave me a six-week crash course at Berlitz. Fortunately, I take to languages easily and didn't find speaking basic Russian too difficult. Reading the Cyrillic alphabet was something else again. The "D" in my last name was a "D" except when it was handwritten; it then became a small "g." The "N" in National Hotel was written as an " H." The abbreviation for the Union of Soviet Socialist Republics in Russian is "CCCP," but in the Russian alphabet, "C" is pronounced like "S" and "P" like "R," to add to the confusion. I soon gave up on reading Russian and relied on my Soviet secretary for translations.

It came as a revelation to me when I arrived in Moscow that with few exceptions, correspondents working there were almost totally ignorant of the Russian language beyond "hello," "please" and "thank you." Even the BBC's correspondent didn't speak Russian. Only a handful had studied Soviet affairs and Russian history.

A working knowledge of the language is vital anywhere but even more so in countries where normal channels of information are closed. Contact with the people is essential to gauge the national mood. This absence of language skills may have been at least partially responsible for Western reporters being caught flat-footed when perestroika and glasnost came to the USSR.

It's quite normal for us to send reporters abroad without studying the required language, but we find it quite inconceivable that some country would send a non-English speaking correspondent to North America.

Much of the blame for this situation can be laid squarely at the doorstep of news management, who select the men and women to report on foreign affairs. Few in management know or care much about foreign reporting beyond war and natural disasters. During my first stint in Moscow, one of my CBC superiors couldn't understand why I ordered supplies from

vv

Helsinki. "If the stuff is available in Helsinki, it's got to be available in Moscow, why pay the freight?" he asked. It suddenly dawned on me that he thought Helsinki was a Soviet city.

The incident reminded me of the foreign editor in Evelyn Waugh's *Scoop* vainly trying to find Reykjavik on the map and allowing how it was jolly difficult knowing where all these places are.

Another story, perhaps apocryphal about the same CBC news executive who had trouble locating Helsinki, was that he thought Shostakovich played for the Green Bay Packers.

When Saigon was falling and North Vietnamese tanks were converging on the doomed city, a *Newsweek* editor in New York got on the phone to one of his photographers to ask if he was out getting shots of the armored columns. He seemed to think the tanks were stopping on the highway for tourist shots.

This abysmal lack of knowledge of foreign affairs among people who are paid to know is not confined to the media. At the height of the cold war, American President Gerald Ford firmly believed that the Soviet satellites of Eastern Europe were independent democracies. (Constantly tripping over his tongue and his feet, Ford became known as "President Polooka" to the press.) As Prime Minister of Canada, Joe Clark (suffering from Jerry Ford disease) obviously had no appreciation of the political sensibilities of the Arab states when he announced (and then quickly withdrew) plans to move the Canadian embassy in Israel from Tel Aviv to Jerusalem. To Clark's credit he grew rapidly in the job to become the most knowledgeable foreign minister since Lester Pearson.

During Expo '67, then-premier of Quebec Daniel Johnson told a high-ranking Soviet visitor that he would like to see Quebec enjoy the same degree of independence within confederation as the Ukraine had within the Soviet Union. Johnson was aware of the visible signs of supposed Ukrainian autonomy—a flag, a constitution, its own foreign minister, even a seat at the United Nations. What he didn't realize was that it was all a facade with no relationship to reality. The Ukraine was at that time an integral part of the USSR under direct control of the Kremlin. When this was explained to him, Johnson conceded that he would not wish to see Quebec in that kind of federation.

This lack of understanding of foreign affairs by government leaders can have dangerous consequences. Hitler launched the Second World War with little or no knowledge of America's war-making potential and invaded the Soviet Union oblivious to the mind-numbing expanse of Russian geography. He, like Stalin and other despotic leaders, rarely travelled beyond his country's borders.

The same myopic and misguided view of the world afflicted Iraq's Saddam Hussein. When President Bush fired his Airforce Chief of Staff for making war-like remarks against Baghdad, Hussein interpreted this as the catalyst that might trigger a military coup against Bush. Republican losses in the mid-term American elections and the ouster of Margaret Thatcher as British Prime Minister were also seen by Hussein as the beginning of a break up of the coalition arrayed against him. Such misreadings are all the more puzzling given the professional international political expertise available to government leaders through their embassies abroad and highly-paid advisors in their foreign ministries. (Saddam Hussein also monitored CNN broadcasts on a daily basis.)

This ignorance works both ways. Early on during my career it came as an ego-bruising shock that the world sees little difference between Canadians and Americans. According to one wag, "Canadians are just decaffeinated Americans." My Soviet translator put it less delicately, "the only difference is that the Americans dress better—they're richer."

On the official level, Canada was, and is invariably seen as being in lock step with Washington. It is in my view, a bad rap. After all, John Diefenbaker refused to play ball with President Kennedy on Cuba, and didn't Pierre Elliott Trudeau decree a new foreign policy motto, "To stand not so high perhaps but always alone?"

It was a policy Brian Mulroney failed to build on resulting in a reinforcement of Canada's image abroad as Uncle Sam's junior partner. Canadians themselves project this image and should not be surprised to discover this attitude when they travel abroad as Ron Rempel did, when he visited Baghdad just before the Gulf War on a church peace mission. He was dismayed to feel himself, as a Canadian, "being lumped with American policy." Dismayed perhaps, but why surprised? He was a Canadian member of a group whose trip was sponsored by Christian Peacemaker Teams of Chicago.

Correspondents are all too often chosen for the wrong reasons. These run the gamut from friend of the editor; someone having a prominent name but little or no reporting experience; a redundant management type in need of something to do; a maturing journeyman reporter with adequate ability and proven loyalty whose promotion to the foreign corps propels him or her to their level of incompetence; to consolation prize for the runner-up in a management competition. The list goes on. Too rarely is the candidate chosen for his or her expertise or the dozen or so attributes that go into the making of a good foreign reporter. It's beginning to change.

The ideal person for the job should have an affinity for, and love of, foreign languages; see the world as part of his or her backyard but with

vv

an appreciation of where your country fits into the global chessboard; be cosmopolitan by nature with a love of foreign literature and culture; and possess the unquenchable sense of curiosity and adventure of a modern-day Marco Polo. "Foreign correspondents," says veteran reporter Jack Cahill, "are bound together in camaraderie and driven by a need to communicate."

That communication must be done with prose that is both substantive and easily comprehended. To compete with the deluge of local and national news that lands on editors' desks the foreign reporter must tighten a story with machine-like precision to fit the allocated space. Reporters who lack these attributes invariably fail as foreign correspondents.

I recollect at least four such instances. In one case a CBC reporter was chosen as the corporation's man in Bonn. Paradoxically, this particular man had an abiding distrust and dislike of Germans, apparently residual sentiment left over from WW II. Predictably his usefulness as a correspondent in Germany was severely limited. One can only wonder why he would have applied for the job in the first place and more importantly how such a serious flaw in a reporter escaped detection during the interview screening process. Not only was this correspondent's tour of duty cut short, but the bureau itself was closed. It would be another 25 years before the CBC reopened its German bureau, this time in Berlin.

The same CBC news chief who didn't know where Helsinki was, was addicted to offbeat feature TV stories. There was just such a reporter on the Prairies who excelled at features and hit the jackpot with a story about research on polar bears at Churchill, Manitoba. Part of the research involved having the bears walk and run on giant caged treadmills to measure heart rates and the like. The story was well written, expertly filmed and fascinating to watch, but hardly the clincher for selecting the reporter as CBC's Asia correspondent.

After a long string of forgettable feature items from the Far East more suitable for travelogues than hard news, our hero was assigned to cover the final months of the Vietnam war. Filming caged polar bears in Manitoba was one thing. Covering the crucial battle for Da Nang was quite another. This dangerous task was left to the field producer and a courageous film crew while the reporter attempted to write the story from the safety of him room in the Caravelle Hotel back in Saigon. Mercifully his foreign reporting career concluded with the fall of Saigon a few weeks later.

(His case is reminiscent of another Waugh character who got a foreign posting because he happened to be on the scene when an aristocratic

London lady got her foot caught in an elevator, giving his paper a scoop on the story.)

Courage and coolness under pressure are key attributes of successful foreign correspondents and camera crews. I remember a most embarrassing incident some years ago in Cyprus when hostilities appeared imminent between Greeks and Turks. A plane was dispatched to remove dependents of British servicemen on the island and reporters who wished to leave. While the embarkation was being filmed by a news crew, the cameraman wouldn't believe what he was seeing through the lens—his reporter elbowing his way past women and children to get a seat on what he thought was the last flight out of town.

Another acquaintance of mine was a first-rate investigative reporter for a major Canadian daily. With sleuth-like diligence and perseverance he tracked down key figures involved in blockbuster stories revolving around union racketeering and suspected espionage. His reward was an international posting to Rome, and journalistic oblivion. European politics, especially the monotonous rise and fall of Italian governments, was no match for the cops 'n robbers excitement he loved and was obviously so good at. He came back to Canada, but for some reason he had lost his investigative touch and faded into obscurity.

Occasionally appointments made on the basis of unusual criteria defy all odds to produce outstanding correspondents. Some years ago, the Toronto *Globe & Mail* chose John Fraser, its dance and art critic, as correspondent to Beijing. It was an unlikely choice. But Fraser proved the critics wrong by becoming one of the most perceptive reporters the paper had ever sent to China. On the downside, because of his lack of a hard news background, Fraser allowed himself to become an active participant in the pro-democracy movement he was covering instead of remaining the dispassionate professional observer.

No less a personage than the late Edward R. Murrow slipped into journalism through the back door. Murrow was, as has often been said, the right man in the right place at the right time. But the fact that he was the CBS man in London when Hitler began running amok in Europe was a sheer accident.

Murrow got the job in 1937 when the network's first choice, a polished gentleman by the name of Fred Willis, turned it down. It was a non-journalistic administrative position calling for someone with erudition, elegance and a touch of class that would impress the elitist English.

Murrow was such a man. He impressed the British with his courtly Southern manners, but he impressed his bosses in New York more when he was pressed into service to report on the ominous developments in Europe to an anxious, war-leery America. What Murrow initially lacked in journalistic expertise he more than made up for with unparalleled skills as a communicator. He was a natural on that relatively new medium called radio. "No other broadcast journalist," wrote David Halberstam in *The Powers That Be*, "would ever again accumulate the prestige both inside and outside the company that Murrow had."

Could he have done it during a different time at another place? Probably not. The lines between good and evil were so indelibly drawn during WW II that no one in Murrow's audience was the least bit critical of his whole-hearted support and active participation in the battle to save Western civilization. Indeed, he verbalized the sentiments of his listeners never having to worry about balance. Winston Churchill was a hero and Murrow said so. The notion that Hitler might be entitled to equal time (which he was not) never even entered his mind. That approach was acceptable, perhaps even required during the war, but in more normal times the lines between good and evil become blurred. Stories seldom present themselves in such stark black-and-white terms.

As in the case of most professions where people become overnight successes, a few of the basics are invariably skipped. Murrow was never able to appreciate the journalistic principle of balance. He was particularly inflexible when another perspective was added, especially if it was done for little more than cosmetic effect. He continued to interpret events and see people as he had during the war—good and evil, right and wrong. (He once compared balancing viewpoints to giving the views of Judas Iscariot equal weight with those of Jesus Christ.)

These cases bring up the old argument about whether reporters should major in journalism or concentrate on English and the humanities. A humanities curriculum obviously gives reporters the necessary grounding to report intelligently on international affairs. Journalism training gives them an appreciation of the importance of professional discipline, but very little background in foreign affairs. With the exception of graduate programs, little progress has been made in integrating the two approaches. If this could ever be achieved journalism would take a giant leap towards the academic respectability and acceptance it so desperately seeks. Before this can happen academics must respect the process by which journalism is created, and place less emphasis on the theoretical social effects of what the news media say and how they disseminate information.

Selecting a journalist for international work is a tricky business. A good résumé helps, but it's no guarantee of success. The successful foreign reporter is someone who wants to be in the "big show," an individual who wants to see, feel and hear history being made. Peter Jennings, one of my former co-anchors at CTV, is such a journalist.

vv

Peter's credentials were not impressive when he became a parliamentary reporter and co-anchor on CTV's newly launched national news in 1962. After dropping out of high school, he worked briefly as a disc jockey. His broadcasting experience when he came to CTV news consisted of that stint as DJ on a Brockville radio station, host of a Saturday afternoon teen dance party and playing the role of a corpse on a CBC drama.

News reporting didn't come easily to Jennings. Experienced reporters find covering Parliament Hill a daunting task. Jennings had never written a line of newscopy in his life. He was, however, a near-flawless newsreader. His smooth delivery and youthful good looks caught the eye of ABC-TV news executives in New York who were scouting around for someone who could pull the struggling network's evening newscast to an acceptable level of respectability. ABC's ratings were so bad that a joke making the rounds at CBS and NBC at the time was, the best way for Washington to keep a state secret was to tell ABC news—the implication being of course that nobody watched it. ABC saw Jennings, at 26, as the news anchor who could lure the Pepsi generation into watching news. The new "anchor boy," as his more mature colleagues called him, failed to measure up to ABC's expectations. His youth, inexperience and lack of depth were all too obvious. Jennings realized he had put the cart before the horse and relinquished the job, yielding to a more mature correspondent.

One of his co-workers at CTV who later became his field producer at ABC predicted Jennings would get out of news to strike it rich as a "Bet Your Ass" kind of game show host. Instead, he became one of ABC's most successful foreign correspondents.

Peter was determined to learn the reporting game from the ground up. Never reluctant to ask co-workers, even junior ones, for help, he honed his writing and interviewing skills. He read voraciously on foreign affairs and became comfortably knowledgeable if not expert on the turbulent politics of the Middle East. Jennings combined the results of his homework with inborn attributes of curiosity, a love of adventure and a zest for a good story, and turned these into a first-class international reporting career. A list of his datelines would read like the index of a Rand McNally atlas.

Eventually, Jennings accomplished what he and the ABC brass had hoped for in 1964. After a 20-year absence, he went back to his old anchorman's chair and catapulted ABC's news ratings to the number one spot. It cost him two marriages, but he did make that fortune. And not by being a game show host either.

vv

Another of my colleagues at CTV was Harvey Kirck. Kirck had a face and a physique more suitable for the wrestling ring than a TV anchor desk. The fact that he wasn't just another pretty face didn't seem to bother his viewers. He stolidly read the CTV National News for 20 years either as anchor or co-anchor. Unlike Jennings, he never developed a knack for reporting and by his own admission found national and international affairs a deadly bore.

Harvey says he could never take the Parliamentary Press Gallery seriously and what went on in parliament was often of no consequence beyond a 40-mile radius of Ottawa. This at a time when Canada was in the throes of political convulsions. The hapless Diefenbaker administration had imploded months before and the highly vaunted Pearson administration turned out to be the gang that couldn't shoot straight. Instead of bringing order out of the chaos left behind by the Conservatives it became mired and enmeshed in a deluge of scandals enlarged by its own stupidity and bungling.

The years on Parliament Hill that Kirck found so "deadly boring" were for Peter Newman the years in which we as a nation were "enduring the pains of passage from the safety of the past to we knew not what." The period was a time of transition that would shape our national character for decades to come. Few in the Press Gallery could articulate what was happening during that period as eloquently as Newman but all of us knew instinctively that the country was going through a change of life. It was an exciting time to be in news—particularly television which, according to Newman, was "revolutionizing the way the public perceived politics and the political process itself." It was during these years that Kirck's brief career as a correspondent on Parliament Hill came to what he calls "a merciful end."

Kirck's first foreign assignment came shortly after he joined the CTV national news team, then based in Ottawa. It was a Commonwealth Conference in London. The British Commonwealth of Nations was coming apart at the seams. A few years earlier, on Canada's insistence, South Africa had been kicked out because of its apartheid policies. Britain herself was losing interest, having decided to throw in its lot with the European Community. That left traditional trading relations among the Commonwealth states, most of them poor Third World countries in limbo. There was lots to write about and a lot of people to talk to for backgrounders and non-attribution if nothing else, but Harvey told us on his return he couldn't for the life of him find anything to report. On one newscast, under pressure from the desk to "send something—please," he simply read the main points of a briefing session communiqué ending with, "like I told you, not much news from today's meeting."

vvv

Kirck was a talented and capable television anchorman who felt more comfortable reading the news than gathering it. The irresistible desire to be in on that big show, to see, feel and hear history being made and tell the story to as many people as possible simply wasn't there.

During my many years in the business I've been privileged to have been associated with many correspondents who had the "right stuff" and then some. Here are just a few of them; Michael Maclear, who worked with both CBC and CTV, the CBC's Joe Schlesinger, John Gray of the *Globe & Mail*, Ben Tierney and Christopher Young of *Southam News* and Arthur Kent, formerly of NBC News and Kitty McKinsie.

All of these correspondents, and there are many others like them, have been in the field a long time and have demonstrated not only journalistic professionalism but the physical and mental stamina required to stand up to killer schedules.

Commendable as staying power is for the foreign correspondent, it isn't prudent to stay abroad indefinitely. William Shirer recalls a colleague and friend who stayed in Central Europe too long. He never went home to renew his roots, gradually putting down new ones in "the worst weedy patches of Mitteleuropa." In the end he became a stranger to his native land and a radio propagandist for the Nazis.

For the would-be correspondent it is equally dangerous to stay a city-side, provincial or even national reporter too long. If you do, says veteran reporter Bill Touey, "You'll become typecast. The paper (or broadcast company) will chew you up and spit you out."

The born foreign correspondent will never be content to cover the routine of city hall or a legislature. He or she is driven by an unconfined curiosity about what is going on in the world and a desire to give the public a ringside seat at the world stage. To do so, this particular breed of reporter is willing to risk being blown up by a land mine on a remote dirt road in a country his editor might be hard pressed to find on the map and with a name the public can't even pronounce.

A retired bush pilot once told me that flying in the Canadian North is 90 percent routine and 10 percent sheer terror. But, he wouldn't have missed the experience for the world. Foreign reporting is something like that. In between the "bang bang" stories are the interviews with prime ministers, presidents, movie stars, heroes, villains, rogues and saints. There are stories on vineyards in Germany, mineral water in France, truffles in Italy and mushrooms in the forests of Russia. It's all part of a glorious mix of being privileged to witness and report history.

The job is particularly challenging for the television correspondent who must have reportorial skills, write well, be knowledgeable about video shooting and editing—and be a performer who can tell a complex

vv

story in a minute and a half. A weak link anywhere along this chain of talent will show up on the screen like the proverbial sore thumb.

The demands of the TV reporter don't end there. Peter Trueman, a veteran of both television and print journalism, puts it this way in his book *Smoke & Mirrors.* The television reporter, unlike his colleague on a newspaper, has only one chance to be right. If a newspaperman fails to isolate the most important elements in the story and get them into his lead paragraphs, he has a chance to recover. His emphasis may be wrong, but he will probably have included the important feature . . . somewhere in the body of the piece. An alert deskman can still save his bacon, by spotting the real news, and moving it up to the top of the story.

Radio reporters can cover themselves too by filing three or four reports with different leads, confident that one will hit the spot.

Television reporters perform the journalistic trapeze act without benefit of a safety net. He or she either extracts the germ of the story off the top on the first go around or falls wide of the mark. Television reports by their very nature are put together with the precision of a Swiss watch. And once the pictures, words and sound are in place, they are not easily disassembled.

As a television reporter, I've always admired camera crews. To my mind they are the unsung heroes of the business. Any TV reporter separated from his camera crew is a forlorn soul indeed. Without them, we couldn't function. In tight situations reporters can crouch, flatten out on the ground or hug a wall. The cameramen have to be close to the action, more or less upright, and subsequently exposed if they are going to get the picture. Under ideal conditions, they've got to think about a dozen details at a time—buttons, dials, lenses, exposures, etc. must all be set correctly for focus and changing light conditions. In hostile situations there is the added stress of personal safety.

In nearly 30 years of television reporting I've worked with scores of camera crews from a dozen countries. During that time, I've only been let down by two cameramen. Once a cameraman refused to accompany me to the site of an armed confrontation between the RCMP and a band of heavily armed Indians near Cache Creek, B.C. The same cameraman also declined to board a military aircraft searching for shipwreck survivors in the Pacific off Vancouver Island because he judged the weather conditions to be unfavorable. In the other case a cameraman chose not to shoot strikers on a picket line when the situation was turning ugly. I'm not condemning these men. Every reporter and cameraman must weigh the risks of every situation and make the decision to go or not to go based on his or her evaluation. People with a low-risk threshold however, should look for another line of work.

vvv

Cameramen as a group are, if nothing else, eccentric and temperamental fellows. Several stand out in my mind. One is Phil Pendry. Phil was based in London. Whenever I worked in the U.K., Ireland or on the Continent, we'd invariably be teamed up. Phil was short and bald except for a monk-like fringe of hair around the back and sides of his head. A cold cigarillo was clenched in his teeth from morning until night. He certainly didn't look like a ladies' man—but in his case, looks were deceiving. He had a disconcerting habit of bringing gorgeous female companions over with him from England on our news assignments. I say disconcerting because after a few weeks on the road away from the comforts of home, grudging admiration from our Cassanova colleague began to turn into something resembling envy. Phil's cosy travel arrangements came to an abrupt end when the CBC accountants discovered that the costs for his lady travelling companions had been hidden under "equipment transportation—excess baggage."

Phil was meticulous about his appearance. His bald pate was carefully powered every morning. His painstakingly manicured toes, weather permitting, protruded from leather sandals, or Jesus shoes, as he called them. Whether filming riot police tossing tear gas canisters in Nuremberg or sniper fire in Belfast, Phil managed to emerge without so much as a smudge on his sockless sandalled feet—and with his unlit stogie firmly in place.

Another cameraman who came under the unforgettable character category was Vancouver-based Graham "Sam" McMullin. Sam worked with me while I was responsible for news coverage for British Columbia and Yukon. Actually our beat extended all the way from Tijuana to Point Barrow, Alaska and all points in between. Sam was a worrier and a perfectionist who agonized over every shot. He was also absent-minded. He was the kind of guy who would end up in the Alaska oil fields in the dead of winter without heavy socks or sweater, yet half a dozen silk ties would be neatly tucked into the corner of his suitcase.

Sam also believed in something called retribution. I was never quite sure how it worked and Sam didn't talk about it much. As best I could figure, he was convinced every time he transgressed God was bound to get him for it. The way to get around divine retribution was to do penance and Sam's way of doing penance was to punish himself before God got around to it with something worse. Sometimes he'd fill his backpack with rocks and like a modern day Sisyphus hike up the steep slopes of Black Mountain with his punishing load. Other times he'd make atonement at work. Once while shooting aerials in a rugged mountain range, he asked our helicopter pilot to make sure his seat belt was secure, then made him take off the passenger side door. Once airborne, he asked the pilot to bank

vv

the craft. With his feet firmly braced against the floor boards, the seat belt cutting into his gut, Sam and his heavy shoulder-harnessed camera hung suspended in the sky over towering mountain peaks. He got the bird's eye shots he wanted and proved to the Almighty that he had the nerve to do it. He and God were even again. Except for occasional lapses Sam had what every good correspondent needs to do the job properly—just the right dose of caution carefully balanced with a feeling of fatalism mixed with an exhilaration of being in on a good story.

I'm sure every television correspondent has had ambivalent feelings about working with field producers. Time was when reporters dug up the story themselves, flushed it out with the relevant facts and delivered it to film, tape or live. Today, likely as not, the correspondent will be second-guessed every step of the way by a field producer who is seldom a journalist and is more interested in production values than news values. Field producers do, however, make day-to-day life for correspondents easier by taking care of distracting details like car rentals, chartering planes, reserving hotel rooms, satellite feeds and studio time. Looking after these housekeeping chores gives the correspondent more "think time," already made scarce by today's instant technology which allows little or no time for thoughtful reporting and comment. The trick is to hang on to the story, and not let the field producer run away with it.

I've always been of the opinion that it's essential for foreign correspondents to dress well. It's hard enough dealing with self-important diplomats and people in authority without looking like someone out of *Front Page*. The days of Runyonesque characters in sloppy suits, scuffed shoes and limp fedoras are long gone. You don't have to look like a model out of *Gentlemen's Quarterly* or *Vogue*. but you should, when the occasion demands, be a sartorial match for any ambassador or cabinet minister. If you don't you could be sent around to the service entrance.

Some correspondents don't socialize. They shun cocktail parties, receptions and dinner invitations. Consequently, they don't entertain in return. The reason professed for professional aloofness is the desire to remain at arm's length with the people they write about. Keeping a distance is fine, but putting yourself out of reach is quite another. As often as not, these correspondents isolate themselves because they feel uncomfortable in social situations.

Formal dinners hosted by the heads of state, ambassadors or business tycoons can be intimidating affairs. Thirty foot candle-lit tables are laid out like felled, fully-decorated Christmas trees. The silver spreads out in serried ranks to the east, west and north of each table setting like so many sterilized surgical instruments awaiting the expert touch of the heart

vv

surgeon. For most of us a handbook of do's and don'ts for formal occasions is a must for navigating through social minefields.

How often and indeed whether journalists are invited to the more formal soirees depends on the individual's prominence and that of his paper or broadcasting network. Reporters and columnists who are, or are thought to be, in possession of some hot information get high priority on the diplomatic dinner circuit. But only a handful of reporters achieve star status on the blue ribbon invitation lists. Those who do frequently feel like the fellow who gets invited to all the parties because he plays the piano, not because he's one of the "in crowd." Rank and file reporters must be content to mingle with the mighty and near-mighty at cacophonic cocktail parties and national day receptions. Little in the way of hard information is gleaned from these gatherings, but they do help to make contacts and pick up on story leads. The trick is to pass up the booze tray and stick to soda water.

Too much drink has ruined too many of my reporter colleagues. The most notable of them was Norman Depoe. Norman was the CBC's chief Ottawa correspondent. He had the uncanny ability of distilling the important part of a complex story and writing the story with just the right number of words in the right order. The clarity and simplicity of his reports more than compensated for his raspy voice which he had abused over the years with too many cigarettes and too much whiskey. That combination ended prematurely, first his career, then his life.

Depoe stories abound. In January 1964, Norman and I were part of the Ottawa-based press contingent accompanying Prime Minister Pearson to a meeting with President Charles De Gaulle in Paris. The visit included a formal reception at the Elysée Palace for the Prime Minister, Mrs. Pearson and the Canadian entourage. Incidentally, when it comes to gala state events no one comes close to matching the French. This one, even though it was a fairly routine affair by French standards, was no exception. A metre-wide red carpet ran from a street gate to a palace vestibule entrance. The entire courtyard was lit up like a football field. Republican Guardsmen in blue tunics and white breeches spaced ten feet apart along the entire length of the carpet snapped briskly to attention as each guest stepped from a car. From inside, the music of the Guards' own symphony orchestra wafted over the scene. All decked out like so many Fred Astaires in white tie and tails entering the sound stage for a 1930s Busby Berkely Hollywood extravaganza, we were soon jolted back to reality. The entrance to the anteroom just off the reception hall was partially blocked by guards in somewhat less splashy uniforms, obliging guests to enter one at a time. As I looked to my right, I came face to face with the business end of a submachine gun protruding from under the cape of a

vv

tough little guardsman who couldn't have stood more than five foot two. Our illustrious host was not universally loved by all Frenchmen. There was still a lot of anger in the country over De Gaulle's alleged sell out by granting Algeria independence. So much anger in fact that De Gaulle was still being targeted for assassination by disgruntled factions within his own military.

Given this intense political atmosphere in the French capital, it wasn't surprising that security men kept a vigilant eye on their president as he and Madame De Gaulle led the Pearsons toward the assembled guests in the main ballroom. When the imperious figure of the General appeared, the crowd parted like the Red Sea to make way for the official party. Everyone that is, except for an obviously tipsy Norman Depoe, World War II medals clanking as he swayed back and forth shakily, standing his ground to greet De Gaulle. Security agents sprang into position. Looks of impending horror crossed the faces of the Prime Minister and his aides. The rest of us, knowing Depoe, steeled ourselves for the calamitous embarrassment about to ensue. It didn't happen. Fresh from a state dinner where wine and champagne had flowed freely, a smiling De Gaulle extended his hand and pointed to Depoe's war medals. In response to a query I couldn't hear, Depoe stiffened to attention and barked, "Oui, Mon Général." After several minutes of animated conversation Depoe stepped back into the crowd and, still smiling, De Gaulle moved on.

Of course the French President had nothing to fear from the Canadian press contingent. The same couldn't be said for the gold plated silver on the buffet tables. On his way out of the palace, security men relieved one of our number of a gold knife and fork he'd tucked into his inside jacket pocket.

Official media receptions are rarely as grand as the Elysée Palace affair. During the Kennedy-Pearson summit meeting in Hyannisport, presidential press officer Pierre Salinger hosted the media in a huge tent pitched on a Massachusetts beach. Jeans and sneakers were the required dress for the evening, although none of us had brought any. We spent a large part of the evening emptying sand out of our dress shoes. The 11-course meal served on mismatched china and in plastic ice cream pails made up in content what it lacked in style. "Here come the CLAMS!" proclaimed an elaborately printed menu, "So roll up your sleeves, Brother, 'cause this is work, only it's spelled F-U-N." At the end of the two-page menu a "P.S. Did you have your bib on? We certainly hope so." The dinner was indicative of the informality and congeniality President Kennedy and his staff cultivated and enjoyed with the media.

Another memorable meal was one hosted by a regional chieftain in the Iraqi desert near Mosul. Low slung tables groaned under the weight of

vv

whole barbecued sheep complete with heads and eyes. The organs, considered prime delicacies, had been left inside the gutted sheep. Anxious to please, my host rolled up his shirt sleeves and was soon elbow deep in the cooked carcass. The more succulent items, totally unrecognizable to me, were extracted with great flourish and ceremoniously and generously deposited on my plate.

Territorial integrity is always jealously guarded by foreign correspondents. I too, was always uneasy when a fellow CBC reporter came into my bailiwick and I know any correspondent worth his salt felt the same way—and it didn't matter whether the interloper happened to be your best friend. Newsrooms may have had a very good reason for sending another correspondent onto your turf, but that didn't make it any easier to swallow. What really stuck in my craw was when these "in and outers," happened to be the high power glory boys from Toronto or Ottawa out to cream off some quick publicity on a hot story. Not only were you expected to brief them on what was going on but also more or less obliged to entertain them as well. Then, likely as not, they landed an interview with the state leader or key minister you'd been working on since you arrived at your posting. For the visiting TV star it was invariably an on camera intro and extro in front of an easily recognizable landmark, then back to Toronto or New York, leaving the resident correspondent to carry on with the daily grind.

For all their antipathy toward these interlopers, foreign correspondents tend to have good rapport with their rivals. They like to bunk with the bunch in the same hotel, dress the same, (bush jackets and variants on the same are always popular) and drink at the same bar. The camaraderie, especially in dangerous situations, is similar to that of soldiers in the field. There's a feeling of fatalism mixed with an "all for one, one for all" exhilaration; a pride in sharing dangers with some of the best people in the business. I suppose it's a "warmth of the herd" mentality, but it also has its practical side. Information is sometimes so scarce reporters have to share what they get so they can put together a story. Besides, correspondents feel uneasy if they can't keep a close eye on what their rivals are up to. People not in the business have no idea of the bottomless despair experienced by a correspondent who gets scooped on a story, not to mention the wrath of editors back home.

Not all correspondents hang out together. There are the inevitable loners who, much to the consternation of the pack, prefer to work on their own. Gordon Sinclair, in his day as a roving foreign correspondent during the thirties, was one who never hung around with other reporters. He claimed that correspondents do tend to use their drinking buddies as experts with the result that everybody at the bar ends up with the same

vv

story. There's some truth to that. But from my experience it's the loner who burns out the fastest. It happened to Sinclair. When his paper *The Toronto Star* asked him to go to Ethiopia to cover the Italian invasion, he refused. He had, says his biographer Scott Young, "seen too much death, starvation, fighting and bad food. He had the adulation of fans, but no personal social life." He was the victim of burnout.

For their own protection, correspondents don't like to differ too much from what their colleagues are saying. If they do, it prompts queries from the desk about who's right and who's wrong.

I recall an instance when I filed an exclusive on French demands that Canadian air squadrons based in France relinquish their nuclear role. It meant a change to photo reconnaissance missions for the Canadians with eventual transfer to Germany and a resumption of a nuclear capability there. Anticipated congratulations from my CTV editors in Ottawa weren't forthcoming. The line up editor asked instead, "If it's such a hot story why hasn't Canadian Press got it?" Therein lies the dilemma correspondents often face. Well-paid reporters are sent abroad, given generous allowances and travel budgets, yet editors get nervous when they don't echo the line of lower paid news agencies. If the correspondent is at odds with what the "wire" says, editors tend to assume their man must be wrong.

Getting a story can be easier than getting it out. There's a Murphy's Law of journalism that states, "the hotter the story the poorer the technical facilities to file it." At times, transmission facilities are non-existent. In times of crisis such as invasions, wars, or other forms of chaos, normal channels of communications through a post office, telegraph office, telex, fax facilities and good old-fashioned phone lines may be cut. Your embassy, if there is one, might come to your aid, but don't count on it, especially if it's a Canadian embassy. They have a reputation for being unco-operative with the media, including their own.

When all communication out of Prague was cut during the Soviet invasion in 1968 all Western embassies, including the normally correct Swiss, helped their correspondents get out dispatches. Only the Canadians refused to bend the rules under extraordinary circumstances, forcing Canadian correspondents to throw themselves on the mercies of the Americans and British. The Americans were particularly helpful.

Technology has eliminated most of the filing frustrations for both print and broadcast journalists. Word processors are now electronically linked to newsrooms and videotape has done away with problematic film processing. Satellites have replaced air connections, giving reporters instant access to newsrooms from virtually any point on the globe.

vv

Nevertheless these facilities are vulnerable to arbitrary denial, and transmissions that are permitted may be subject to censorship.

Restrictions on editorial freedoms don't begin and end with the censors. Often the fiercest fights are with the desk back home. Correspondents, TV reporters in particular, are kept on an increasingly short leash these days. Editorial control is so tight, reporters are obliged in some instances to file stories tailored to the perceptions and biases of "desk men" whose thinking has been heavily influenced by the agency copy and what they've read in the *Globe & Mail* or the *New York Times*. The television reporter's frustration is further compounded by the fact that editorial people with little or no reporting expertise emphasize production over journalism. The product that emerges is a slick, homogeneous newscast with little to differentiate it from half a dozen others on the tube.

The room for distortion on television, and to a lesser extent radio, is immense. Because of time constraints the qualifying statements of newsmakers are sometimes deleted, sentences are edited in juxtaposition with unrelated sentences, an innocent face is edited over incriminating words. All can distract and do serious damage to the truth. If, as statistics suggest, 80 percent of people rely almost exclusively on TV for their news, editors and producers have a heavy responsibility to handle a correspondent's material with professional care and diligence. Correspondents, however, should not consider their material sacrosanct. Today's major stories are invariably interconnected and the journalist in the field sees only a small part of the bigger picture. It is up to the editors to inject the required balance and objectivity.

A continuing dilemma for the Canadian news media is their heavy dependence on American sources for foreign news—including news from the United States itself. Most of the foreign news appearing in Canadian newspapers, radio, and television concerns American issues. As the neighbor of a superpower, whose actions usually impact directly on Canada, that's not surprising. What is perplexing is that Canadians depend almost totally on American sources for the American news carried by our media.

According to a survey published by *Content* magazine, a mere 11 percent of news stories from across the border is supplied by Canadian reporters. The consequences of this go beyond the annoyance of reading copy peppered with American terms and definitions. It's disquieting for Canadians to hear the American president referred to as *the* president and Indian reserves called "reservations." The American copy may refer to terrorists. The same people in Canadian copy are called protestors. Because of its sheer volume, the American copy wins out and Canadians develop an American outlook on the world. This American slant on the

vvv

news will continue and become even more pervasive as Canadian editors and media owners take the cheap and easy way out.

How do we stack up with other countries? According to U.S. Information Agency figures, not very well. At any given time Canada has about 25 full-time correspondents in the United States. That is five times less than Brazil and half as many as Italy. The Germans have 90 correspondents in New York alone. The Japanese have 150 in that American city. Cheap, readily available, attractively-packaged news using a common language means that Canadian media operations will continue to be tempted to put profit ahead of national responsibility. An absence of the Canadian viewpoint will be with us for the foreseeable future and be a continuing threat to our Canadian identity. Indeed, the threat is global. Cable Network News (CNN) is watched worldwide via satellite. Once it begins broadcasting in other languages besides English, the "American viewpoint" will penetrate every major culture on earth.

The next decade will see drastic changes in the way international reporters work. The bureau structure itself faces a complete overhaul if not total elimination. The Gulf War showed not only how rapidly an army can be deployed, but also how quickly news teams can be put in place. That rapid deployment capability will make it unnecessary to have fully manned bureaus around the world. Many news organizations, even the rich television networks can no longer afford them anyway. According to ABC news chief Roone Arledge, the bureaus aren't as important as they once were. He says, "You still have to get out and cover the story, but you don't have to be on location all the time."

The traditional events-of-the-day nightly national network news shows which rely so heavily on their bureaus may also be on the way out. All-news channels like CBC's News World in Canada and CNN in the United States, with its global reach, mean viewers have constant access to international events from many different sources. This, combined with the international news local outlets glean from network syndication, plus independent news service material incorporated into their supper hour programs, is making the glamorous network evening show redundant. This is increasingly true of the national newscasts on CBC and CTV in Canada. By 9 or 11 o'clock viewers have seen, heard or read it all.

The trend, in television at least, is two-fold. There is a shift toward more magazine-oriented and analytical network news programming, like Ted Koppel's *Nightline*, the CBC's *Prime Time*, and expanded network "wire services," providing affiliates and subscriber stations with a constant 24-hour-a-day flow of news stories which each station can weave into its own newscasts. This kind of service had been the mainstay of radio news for years. There will be foreign correspondents—sort of. As

vv

Arledge points out, under any system, you still have to get out and cover the story. But increasingly, the overseas story will be covered by correspondents based in New York, Los Angeles or Toronto. National and international assignments will become interchangeable. Much of the day-to-day coverage required to feed the news service will be provided by resident free-lancers. The old glory days of the true foreign correspondent are numbered—killed by spiralling costs, editorial emphasis on immediacy rather than depth and not least of all, technology.

What will not change are the demands on journalists to report on increasingly complex issues accurately, fast and in language everyone from school drop out to professor can comprehend.

In the course of their work, foreign correspondents see much anguish, suffering and death. They get more than a passing acquaintance with at least three of the Four Horsemen of the Apocalypse: war, death and famine. Some might even say the first horseman, the false Christ, is no stranger to the business. Given such a working environment, there is always the danger of overreacting to situations by becoming a participant rather than a professional observer.

John Fraser, *Globe & Mail* Beijing correspondent during the heady days of the post-Mao pro-democracy demonstrations, freely admits his personal involvement in the events that shook the Chinese capital. In his book *The Chinese* he writes, "I too found myself caught up in Chinese politics and addressing a gathering of over ten thousand people during the remarkable events at Xidan Democracy Wall."

The CBC's Brian Stewart found his Ethiopian famine assignment so overpowering that he was unable to remain the dispassionate observer. The experience, he says, affected a profound change in his life.

Alongside such overpowering cataclysmic events as famine and war the antiseptic rules and ethics of professional journalism have a way of sounding hollow and meaningless. Yet, journalists have a duty to keep emotionalism in check while at the same time avoiding the use of cynicism as an anaesthetic to deaden normal feelings for the suffering of our fellow man.

If many of us deaden our emotions as a means of self-preservation, I would hazard a guess that few escape at least a tinge of guilt. There's guilt in lying in a warm bed after leaving infantrymen huddled in foxholes enduring relentless artillery fire; in walking away from hollow-eyed children with swollen stomachs to enjoy a well-cooked meal and good French wine. There's guilt when we turn heart-rending tragedies into "good" stories that make the front page or lead the evening television news.

vvv

The CBC's Bill Cameron, a veteran of numerous foreign assignments, writes in *The Newsmakers*, "Maybe the real reporter is not necessarily the most talented, but the one who can survive all this guilt, doubt, shame and suspicion, and get at least part of the story home."

The truth is that the television news business in particular is increasingly trivializing tragedy and human misery. Reams of "hot" footage pouring into the newsrooms is frequently treated like so many vicarious thrills for the armchair news theatre junkies. And, there's the promotion to go with it. FEEL THE HEAT FROM THE MIDDLE EAST exhorts the CBC Newsworld's billboard. GET IT WHILE IT'S HOT says another, words superimposed over a raging fire. Still another shows a blow up of a freeze frame of a frenzied mob of protesters. The words promise LIVE DEMONSTRATIONS hourly. And this from the CBC.

The charge that TV news exploits human suffering can no longer be denied. Toronto writer Simon Houpt says the industry has gone beyond exploitation to "the glorification of exploitation." Writing in the *Globe & Mail*, Houpt accuses TV news, the all-news channels in particular, of steering viewers clear of any issue that requires a long-term commitment. "Like fast food," he writers, "the issues presented stay with us for enough time to cause slight social irritation, not long enough to bog us down with a serious case of moral indigestion."

News (television news in particular) is deteriorating into flashy packages of pre-digested sound bites aimed at entertaining rather that informing. Are journalists becoming ratings hucksters instead of fulfilling their traditional role of society's catalyst for public dialogue of issues that really matter? Tomorrow, today's big story will be as cold as yesterday's mashed potatoes. It is gone. Forgotten. The effect is dealt with by our media, but the cause that gave it birth is shunted aside, allowed to fester and surface again another day. There are new hot stories clamoring to be given their mandatory 45 seconds in the spotlight. Perhaps it's a matter of information overload, but when issues are not dealt with adequately by the media they cannot be confronted and dealt with by society.

Thanks to Star Wars technology, today's television correspondents know how to communicate. They are less certain about what to communicate. The time has come to move beyond glibness and slick packaging. The world is watching, and expecting more.

My journalistic career spanned nearly 35 years. Nine of those years were spent covering politics and national affairs in Ottawa. Other assignments and postings took me to 27 countries. Besides politics and diplomacy, I reported on military matters, scientific achievements, social trends, entertainment, sports, crime and any number of other areas. But it was coverage of armed conflict that left an indelible impression on my

vv

consciousness. Wars are news and no other story stirs the adrenalin like men locked in mortal combat. Some reporters are addicted to the danger of wars and seek them out to get their fix.

I've often heard it said that wars don't settle anything. That's not true. Wars may not be the best way to settle things, but they do determine the fate of leaders, nations, continents as well as economic and social orders.

Reporting on politics and diplomacy, both at home and abroad, has left me with a deep disillusionment about the motives of people in high places. With a few notable exceptions, the words arrogant, ignorant and self-serving come to mind. In a number of more isolate cases I would have to add cruel and callous. This leads me to think of the name Mohammed al Mashat.

I met al Mashat long before he became Saddam Hussein's controversial ambassador to the United States and before he became Canada's best known landed immigrant. In the early seventies when he was a relatively minor functionary in the Iraqi government we were strolling through Baghdad's *souk,* or market. On an impulse I flipped a large somewhat unmanageable Iraqi coin into a beggar's bowl. The broad gap-toothed smile and bow I got in return indicated I had made the man's day. Al Mashat was furious. "Don't do that," he snapped. "You only encourage them."

Little did I suspect that years later, when a war would go badly for Iraq, al Mashat as ambassador to Washington would for all intents and purposes defect, and get fast-tracked into Canada by dipsy-doodling his way to the head of a year-long immigrant waiting list. And what about all those harangues against the coalition allies and apologies for Hussein's murderous behavior? "Just doing my job," he would say, "just doing my job."

Foreign correspondents' lives are full of other incongruities. As witnesses to history at close range, they know that the actual process of history in the making is quite different from that which is presented to posterity.

When I covered the first phase of the Strategic Arms Limitation Talks (SALT) between the Americans and Russians in Helsinki, I spotted one of the Soviet negotiators in the airport lounge. We were waiting for the same Aeroflot flight back to Moscow. He recognized me as one of the foreign press. After some hesitation he approached me to ask a favor. Could I, he wondered, buy a Braun electric shaver for him. He would reimburse me with rubles (practically worthless) which are not accepted outside the USSR. I didn't have enough hard currency myself, so I couldn't help him. But what irony! Here was a man who had just gotten up from the disarmament negotiating table where multi-warhead nuclear missiles worth billions had been traded back and forth like so many poker

vv

chips, virtually begging me to buy him an electric razor unavailable in his own country at any price—even for a highly-placed bureaucrat.

In this business it is easy to slide from healthy skepticism into corrosive cynicism. I don't think I ever did, mainly because I had the privilege of meeting thousands of decent, unselfishly motivated ordinary people in the course of my work. It was, and is my conviction that they are the glue that holds a country—any country—together in spite of the manifest shortcomings of those who hold the reigns of power.

I have written elsewhere in detail about the pros and cons of being a foreign correspondent. At its worst the job can be boring, physically and emotionally exhausting, life-threatening, endlessly frustrating, even humiliating. At its best it can mean being a first-hand observer of events that shape history and change the destiny of the human race for good or ill. Sometimes foreign reporting can be the catalyst that changes things for the better. Not, perhaps, one single reporter's work, but certainly the collective efforts of honest journalists as a whole. Besides, what other job could have given me the opportunity to see the world, walk with the high and mighty and have somebody else pick up the tab?

Epilogue

SINCE I BEGAN WORK ON THIS BOOK WORLD EVENTS have moved at a dizzying pace. So much so, that our thought process circuits have become severely overloaded. A world order, albeit volatile, that seemed so permanent and immutable such a short time ago is no more.

Three new countries, Lithuania, Latvia and Estonia have emerged (or re-emerged) on the world stage. What was left of the seemingly invincible Soviet Empire imploded, clearing the way for the creation of a dozen or so more nations, not to mention the possibility of even these splintering into scores of independent ethnic groupings.

The failed coup of August 1991 by Kremlin hard liners brought the curtain down on the cold war once and for all. And with its demise went all the givens and constants of confrontational East-West ideologies; the polar star by which foreign correspondents had navigated their international beats for 50 years. These events are forcing reporters (as well as foreign policy makers) to sail into uncharted waters.

The meltdown of communism's core is having ramifications throughout the world. The dreaded KGB which for decades made life for correspondents so difficult, and at times dangerous, has been defanged. The new KGB has pledged to disband the network of millions of informants and to make public some hitherto secret files. But the organization itself remains largely intact.

Aftershocks of the three days that shook the world were felt almost instantaneously in the communist strongholds of Asia and in Cuba. It is in these areas where the correspondent corps will now focus much of its attention. How long can Cuba, China, North Korea, Vietnam, Cambodia and Laos continue to impose totalitarian rule at the point of a gun?

The Soviet collapse so spooked the already skittish Chinese that the authorities forbade foreign correspondents based in Beijing from staging their scheduled annual summer bash satirically dubbed the *Peaceful Evolution Summer Ball*. It is an indication that at least for the short term reporters in China will operate on a considerably tighter leash.

The end of the cold war has also left both the architects of international policy and the correspondents who report on foreign affairs with an identity crisis. A "new world order" is evolving, but will it be orderly? Dictatorships are unlikely to go away and totalitarian regimes tend to make for a disorderly place.

vvv

In the wake of the new Russian Revolution one western reporter in Moscow commented that he'd just covered the biggest story of the last half of the 20th century not to mention his career. "After this," he went on, "everything will be anticlimactic. Maybe it's time to get out of this business."

He may have covered the biggest story of his life, but if he leaves now, others may yet have to write the conclusion. Authoritarianism runs deep in the Russian psyche and a return to demagoguery is a constant threat.

It is also becoming increasingly apparent that in the next decade most of the foreign correspondents' dispatches will deal with economics. Europe is now twice its pre-cold war size—with incredible potential for economic growth. Japan continues to gobble up huge chunks of the North American automotive and consumer market. The removal of the Red menace heralds a diminution of American military power in the Pacific, clearing the decks for a newly assertive Japan. How will North America fight back? Global economic supremacy however, says Jacques Attali, president of the European Bank, will not be the main event in the current decade. It will be the confrontation between the rich nations and the have-nots. Instead of the old East-West Iron Curtain, a North-South curtain may form the framework around which foreign news is reported.

For aspiring foreign correspondents, who for generations have cut their teeth on danger and intrigue, this may all sound like unexciting stuff. But for those in need of a regular fix of combat reporting (and there are those) there's little cause for anxiety. At this writing, civil war rages in former Soviet and Yugoslavian republics and tribal violence shows no sign of abating in South Africa. Nor is there any assurance that China's hard liners will cave in as easily as their Kremlin counterparts. The horsemen of the Apocalypse haven't retreated. They're just changing mounts.